HA

GARDENER

HANDYMAN GARDENER

David L. Bebb

OCTOPUS
BOOKS

Contents

First published in 1979

This edition published in 1985 by Octopus Books Limited
59 Grosvenor Street London W1

Reprinted 1986, 1987

ISBN 0 7064 2304 6

Printed in Hong Kong

1 The General Design

THE British, whether proprietors of country estates or cultivators of modest suburban plots, have long been known as a nation of gardeners. Today, with the trend toward home ownership and increased leisure time, the popular enthusiasm for gardening is probably greater and more widespread than ever before.

A garden is more than just a display of attractive vegetation, however lovingly tended and thoughtfully disposed. It consists also of a variety of man-made elements and services that provide the setting for the plants. Many of these elements – paths, driveways, walls, gates, raised beds, terracing, and much else – can be extremely expensive if the work of construction or assembly is done by professionals. This book is designed to enable even the novice to do these jobs himself – and, moreover, to avoid the errors in design or technique that so often mar otherwise attractive gardens.

I have assumed that the gardener is starting from scratch with a newly built house; but the information applies equally to owners of mature gardens who wish, for instance, to replace a fence with a wall, a gravel path with a stone-paved one, a sunken garden with an ornamental pond, and so on.

Objectives

Before setting out to create a new garden, the first question one needs to answer is: What general purposes is it going to fulfil? Most home owners would agree that it should be a place for growing ornamental shrubs and flowers, and perhaps fruit and vegetables, and that it should provide space for sitting in the open air. These are certainly basic elements, but a garden containing such elements can be attractive or unattractive, efficient or inefficient, a pleasure to tend or a tiresome chore.

And these qualities depend greatly on the selection, siting, and grouping not only of the plants themselves but of the man-made elements against which the plants are displayed. Moreover, good design can be used to conceal as well as to reveal. Too often the appearance of an otherwise attractive garden is marred by the careless, last-minute siting of mundane but essential items such as dustbins, rubbish heap, and domestic-fuel tank. Finally, the upkeep of a well-stocked garden inevitably requires a good deal of time and effort, so the design should be as labour-saving as possible. This does not mean, for instance, that one should replace the lawn with a bleak expanse of paved terrace, but that a judicious blend of hard landscaping and greenery will make the garden not only more interesting but a great deal easier to maintain.

Priorities

Builders usually provide little more than the bare essentials outside the house, and if you have moved into a new house you may find that it lacks even a path to the back door. Buying a new home usually leaves one with little cash to spare for anything else. But you will probably want to transform the brown, rubble-strewn wilderness around the house into a living garden as soon as possible. What should your priorities be?

The first should be a proper access and drive, if these are not already provided. It is generally desirable to park vehicles, including visitors' cars, off the road, and if the site is big enough, there should be a space to turn a car around so that one does not have to reverse on to the highway. If a drive and access already exist, it is worth

Hard-surface features in mature gardens. **Above left** Patio with raised bed. **Right** Terrace and pool.

Development of a garden. **Below** Clearing rubble from the site after the builders had left in 1957. **Below right** Marking out a path and lawn boundaries.

questioning whether they are wide enough: although it sounds little, an extra 300 mm (1 ft) on the width of the drive could make it much easier to manoeuvre a vehicle. Dry walk-ways to both the front and back doors are also a top priority, and you may wish to provide dry access to the rubbish bins and clothes line as well.

Next you should consider enclosing the boundaries of the property. Often some form of fencing, perhaps a chain-link fence, will have been provided; although it may not suit your taste it may be as well to make do with it for the time being and allocate money and time to development within the garden. (A quick-growing hedge, incidentally, will soon conceal the boundary features.)

The more ambitious landworks within the garden will take time and physical effort, and a carefully thought out plan is essential before beginning them. Examine the site carefully, checking for evidence of poor drainage, depth of topsoil (if any!), location of sewerage and water pipes, and so on. Topsoil may have been scraped into a hollow during building operations, so it is

Above Ten years after: the garden in 1967. **Left** August 1978: the present garden shows an attractive mixture of mature plantings and man-made features.

worth digging a few trial holes, which will also show if there is a hard pan which might impede drainage.

Many garden sites can be improved with some change of level, but moving soil is an onerous job and it could well be worth hiring a mechanical digger if you plan a large-scale operation. Topsoil is precious and should be carefully put aside before the land form is changed. Avoid, if possible, the expense of having to cart soil away: soil cut from one area can often be used to fill another or to provide an interesting raised area.

It is a good opportunity now to install the garden services such as an underground pipe to a conveniently sited water tap, and maybe an armoured underground electric cable to serve a garden shed or for garden lighting.

Once all the landworks are completed, perhaps a patio built, and all the rubbish cleared away, the garden needs a good double digging and can then be left to weather. Extra topsoil may need to be imported to the under-privileged garden. Only when all this work is complete is it time to form a lawn and plant up the garden.

Design principles

Work out a budget before you begin: the creation of an attractive garden can seldom be done on a shoestring, and it might be worth phasing the development. Also, remember that landscaping on any sort of scale generally consumes a good deal of time.

A good garden begins with planning, not planting, and a scale plan (minimum 1:100) will prove to be most helpful. It not only enables you to estimate quantities of materials needed, but offers less distractions to creative thinking than planning purely on the site. The plan should note the aspect of the property in relation to the sun and the direction of prevailing winds, and should include any existing garden features which you intend to keep.

Before undertaking any building work, check that you will not run foul of the law, particularly in relation to building regulations. This especially

Right Curved edges help to alleviate the angularity of the typical modern garden.

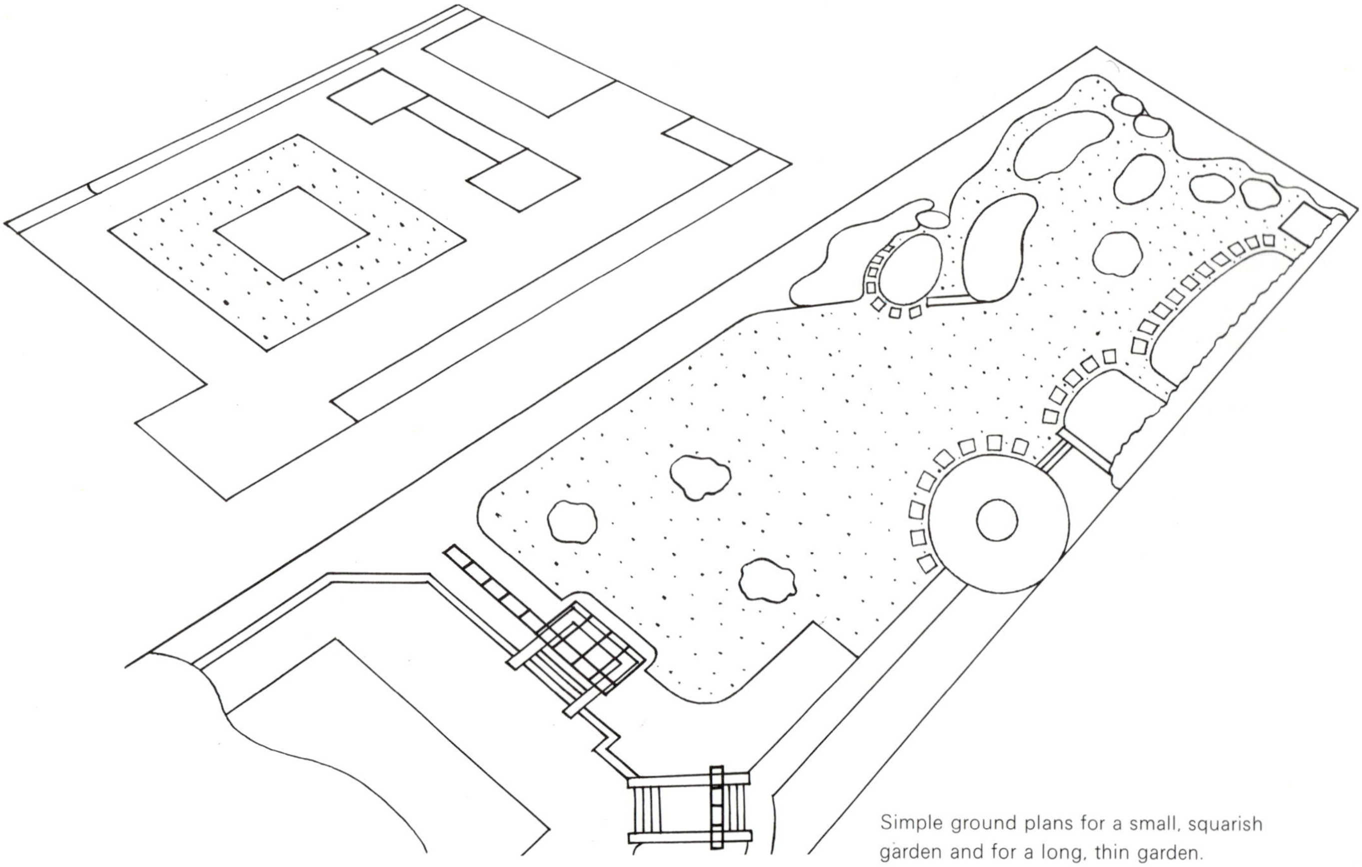

Simple ground plans for a small, squarish garden and for a long, thin garden.

An impression of how the plans opposite could be realized in practice, showing the use of hard and soft surfaces.

Above Installing drainage: 1 Plan view showing main and tributary pipes draining to a sinkhole; 2 Laying pipes, with joints being covered with slate before the trench is filled with coarse aggregate and topsoil; 3 A pipe draining into the sinkhole. **Right** A gap between a lawn and a hard vertical structure makes it easy to cut the lawn edge with mower or trimmer.

applies to boundary walls and fences, and in certain circumstances (such as a tall wall or fence) planning permission may be required – as it will often be, too, for a new entry-way for a car. You will also need permission to install or even to move drains that carry sewerage. If in doubt, be sure to consult your local council. It is also worth checking that there is no restrictive covenant in your house deeds regarding the erection of walls or fences. Finally, it will certainly be in your interest to determine the exact position and ownership of boundary features of your garden, and to talk the matter over with your next-door neighbours before beginning any work.

Plan to hide or camouflage ugly items such as fuel-storage facilities, and screen the dustbin and refuse area and the services – telephone poles, manhole covers, water stand pipes – from the rest of the garden without making them difficult to get at.

Where feasible, attempt to provide shelter from prevailing winds and some degree of privacy. This is particularly important in relation to the siting of a patio.

The secret of an attractive garden is often founded on maintaining interest. It is desirable, although not always possible on a small site, to create concealed areas, so that the eye does not see the whole garden in one glance. This can be done by building subdivisions that have the effect of creating smaller gardens within the main one. If done intelligently this can create the illusion that the garden is bigger than it really is. A similar effect can also be achieved by terracing the garden or creating raised beds.

As a means of mitigating the squareness of most garden sites, curving features such as flower beds, paths, and garden walls can produce a pleasing effect. On the other hand, avoid curving a service path through a lawn just for the sake of novelty; most people will take the shortest route, resulting in worn patches of lawn.

The most important principle of all is that the hard and soft landscape should be integrated, and that the garden structures should help to highlight the growing plants. There should be a sense of harmony throughout. It is almost invariably better if the man-made materials used are mellow in colour: bright, multi-coloured paving slabs and walling materials tend to look garish. Bear in mind, also, the importance of harmonizing related features: a somewhat formal layout tends to look best with a conventional modern house, while much of the charm of an old,

colour-washed country cottage would be destroyed if its garden was walled and pathed with concrete.

These remarks also apply if you are planning to improve an existing garden. The main problem is that there is perhaps not so much scope because one generally wants to preserve some of the existing features. Certainly, healthy, mature trees and other fine specimens and features should be preserved if possible. But it is essential that they are fully integrated into your new design: often it is not so much an individual feature that is beautiful as its relation to the objects around it.

Once the basic needs – access, drive, boundary enclosure, and paths – have been catered for, a significant improvement might well be made with a well-laid-out patio, as an 'extension' to the main living room. The cost of paving a large patio and fitting a door linking the patio and the living room can be considerable. But you may well find that your building society will be prepared to make you a further loan on a mortgage to finance such home improvements.

Other developments may be phased with, for instance, the growth of children. A paved circuit around the garden will be appreciated as a cycle track, while a sand pit – keeping the children amused for hours – can later, perhaps, be converted to a garden pool.

Such improvements, however, often entail a great degree of disruption, with soil and materials littering those areas which are not to be developed. It is as well to provide a 'sacrifice' area, and concentrate materials within it. Access for machinery may need to be considered and fence panels may have to be removed for this purpose.

Man-made features in a typical garden. **Top** Retaining wall made from natural stone. **Centre** Informal flight of steps connecting different levels. **Bottom** Stone flags set at intervals to make a path across a lawn.

2 Garden Walls

Building a wall can be one of the most satisfying of home-improvement jobs. A solid boundary wall gives you privacy; it also costs little to maintain and has sound-deadening qualities. Walls within the garden are used to retain earth where there is a change in land level, as raised flower beds, and to divide up different parts of the garden.

Bear in mind that wall building demands more skill than erecting a fence, as well as considerably more time, effort, and capital outlay. Foundations will be needed, and the wall may need strengthening at intervals and at openings. However, if attractive materials are selected – it is very important, for instance, to match or complement those of the house – and the wall is soundly built, it is possible significantly to enhance the appearance and value of one's property. Finally, of course, a well-built wall will almost certainly last longer and may be more suitable for exposed sites than a fence.

Materials

The choice of materials is a vital decision which can make or mar your whole garden-building project. You have a choice of using bricks, concrete blocks, or natural stone.

Bricks

There are literally hundreds of different varieties of bricks available, but not all of them are suitable for use in the garden. The majority of bricks are made of clay, but concrete and calcium silicate bricks are also available. Clay bricks are classified, basically, according to variety, quality, form and strength.

'Variety' indicates the particular use to which the bricks are to be put. *Common bricks* are fairly dull and uninteresting in appearance. *Facing bricks* have an attractive appearance and are the ones used for the outside of homes. A wide variety of colours and textures is available, some of which weather better than others. You should note that many facing bricks have the special appearance incorporated only onto three of the four brick faces, which may be a problem if you intend to build a thin 100 mm (4 in) 'half-brick-thick' wall with both sides exposed to view. *Engineering bricks* are particularly dense, strong, and water resistant. They are sometimes used for brickwork below ground level, damp-proof courses, or wherever extreme strength and water resistance are necessary, such as in a soil-retaining wall; they are also used for brick paving. Common and facing forms are available.

'Quality' describes the bricks' durability. *Internal* quality should be avoided for the garden and you should use either *ordinary* or *special* quality bricks; the latter can withstand extreme exposure. Engineering bricks are normally of this standard.

'Forms' of brick available include *standard rectangular*, which may be flat and solid, or may incorporate a frog (indentation) which is laid uppermost and filled with mortar, or may be perforated with small holes. There are also *special shapes*, which are available from some manufacturers in the same colour and texture as standards, and which can be used, for example, to round tops of walls and to create interesting finishes.

'Strength' is most important if the wall is loadbearing. There are eight classes of clay brick, class 1 the weakest, class 15 the strongest.

When selecting bricks for the garden, choose those that will blend with the house and surroundings, and check on their frost-resistant qualities. Builders' merchants generally stock only a limited range, and to see what is available it may be worth visiting a building centre in one of the major cities, or the Brick Advisory Centre in London.

Blocks

These are normally of concrete and are available as conventional blocks, in dense or insulating form, and as special types for the garden, such as split facing blocks and screen blocks. Conventional blocks are available in thicknesses from 50 to 225 mm (2 to 9 in); some of the thicker types are hollow and can be reinforced with steel rod embedded in concrete.

Dense concrete blocks are available in plain form, but a number of decoratively surfaced versions have been developed for garden use and house building; some are made from reconstituted stone, often giving a pleasing, mellow appearance.

A brick wall makes a substantial and effective garden boundary. Its hard, flat surfaces will provide an attractive background for borders and can also be used for training plants, such as this wisteria.

Top Bricks are available in many colours, varieties, and forms. **Above** Building materials: split block, split walling, concrete, and local stone. **Above right** Aggregated limestone and sandstone blocks. **Left** Pierced screen blocks.

Split facing blocks are formed by splitting larger blocks which have been made from crushed stone aggregate. Some are sold already split; others the user splits himself immediately before use. Usually these blocks are 70 mm ($2\frac{3}{4}$ in) or so high and 600 mm (24 in) long and are available in a variety of colours. Some are suitable for laying dry.

Pierced screen blocks are available in a wide variety of designs generally forming a geometric pattern when incorporated into the wall. They are usually 300 mm (12 in) square and 100 mm (4 in) deep, and most are sold with matching pier or plaster blocks and coping. Screen block moulds are available for you to make your own, if you have the time.

Natural stone

This can be the most expensive and the most demanding material with which to work, but a carefully fitted stone wall has a beauty that few other materials can match.

The most common building stones are granite, limestone, and sandstone. Granite is very hard and very durable, but it is very difficult to break and chip and is generally unsuitable for garden walls. The easiest to work with are the stratified (layered) rocks such as limestones and sandstones, but their readiness to split, which is an advantage to the builder, also makes them vulnerable to hard winter frosts unless precautions are taken. The most highly regarded of the limestones is the creamy white Portland stone, while the best-known sandstone is the light brown York stone. However, since transport

Right A natural-stone wall laid with mortar.
Below Dry-laid stone wall.

costs are considerable, it makes sense to use stone native to your area. If there are no stone quarries in your district you would be advised to forget a stone wall: stone imported from another area can look incongruous.

There are two classes of stonework: *rubble*, in which uncut stones are fitted together in the 'natural' state; and *ashlar* walling, in which cut stones are laid in fairly regular layers. The latter is inevitably more expensive, and most stone garden walls are of the rubble type, laid with mortar or laid dry.

Quantities of stone required are much more difficult to assess than for other materials. Your supplier should be able to give you a guide, but I have found from experience that 1,000 kg (1 ton) of sandstone will build about 2.5 m² (3 sq yd) of a low rubble wall about 300 to 350 mm (12 to 14 in) thick. Ask for a sample in which the face area of the largest stones is not more than five or six times that of the smaller.

Mortar

This is the gap-filling glue which evens out irregularities in size and shape between bricks, blocks, or stones. Old buildings were built with a mortar of lime and sand which is quite unsuitable today. The modern form has four ingredients: cement, usually ordinary Portland cement; soft, clean building sand (not 'sharp' concreting sand); water; and a plasticizer to make the mix workable and wall-building easier. A good mortar should cling to the trowel and spread smoothly, like butter.

The traditional plasticizer used is hydrated lime, which not only improves workability but prolongs the working time. Many find it convenient to use additives, normally sold in liquid form, which work by entraining small air bubbles and so act as a lubricant. Never use washing-up liquid for this purpose: the alternative to additives is to use masonry cement, which has plasticizing materials already in it.

For brickwork below soil level and for retaining walls in those areas of the country with high-sulphate soils (your local building inspector will advise you). Use a special sulphate-resisting cement instead of Portland cement.

Sometimes an attractive effect can be achieved by adding a proprietary colouring pigment to the mortar. But be cautious about using such pigments: you will have to live with the colour for many years.

The table below gives the recommended mortar mixes for free-standing garden walls and retaining walls:

	Proportions by volume	
	Brick Walls	*Block and Stone Walls*
Cement: lime: sand	$1:\frac{1}{2}:4\frac{1}{2}$	1:1:6
Cement: sand: plasticizer	1:4	1:5
Masonry cement: sand	1:3	1:4

Weaker mixes have less frost resistance. Mixing up and using the mortar should be done with care: measure the ingredients accurately, using buckets. Mix thoroughly, turning the heap over at least three times till an even grey colour is achieved. Make a depression in the middle of the heap and add water sparingly, turning over till a workable mix, not too dry nor sloppy, is achieved. A drier mix is needed for heavy blockwork. If a plasticizer is used, follow the maker's instructions and do not use too much – it can impair the strength of the mortar. Mix no more than you can use in two hours: after this, especially in summer, the mix begins to become unworkable.

Tools

In addition to the basic gardening tools such as spade, shovel and wheelbarrow, you will need the following:

Steel or linen tape 10 m (33 ft) long.
Steel pocket tape
Bricklayer's spirit level
Bricklayer's trowel
Pointing trowel
1 kg (2.2 lb) lump or 'club' hammer
Steel cold chisel
Steel bolster chisel
Heavy-duty plastic buckets for measuring concrete and mortar ingredients (keep one separate for cement)
Builder's rubber gloves (to avoid getting rough hands)
Line, pegs, and builder's pins
Timber straight-edge about 2.5 m (8 ft) long
Builder's square, which is actually a triangle. You can make this from three pieces of wood, each 75 × 25 mm (3 × 1 in) in section, and respectively 900 mm (3 ft), 1.2 m (4 ft), and 1.5 m (5 ft) in length.
Banker board (a large sheet of marine ply or other hard, smooth, waterproof material) for hand mixing or receiving loads from a small mixer. Alternatives are the garage floor or concrete drive surface.
Another, smaller piece of smooth board or sheet metal from which the mortar can be used during the building operations.

A brick wall reinforced with piers.

Building with bricks and blocks

You can build a 100 mm (4 in) thick brick or block boundary wall up to about 600 mm (24 in) high. Above that height the wall will need to be strengthened by piers (regularly spaced thickened sections) or must be built 200 mm (8 in) thick throughout. The thinner and higher the wall, the greater is the number of piers required and the less spacing possible for a given length. For instance, for a 100 mm (4 in) thick wall, the piers should be about 4.5 m (15 ft) apart when the wall is 1.2 m (4 ft) high, and 4 m (13 ft) when it is 1.8 m (6 ft) high. Always ensure that the piers are bonded into the wall by laying some of the bricks transversely.

The first thing that needs to be done is to clear obstructions from the site, including rubble, shrubs, and hedges. At a selected point you may find it convenient to drive in a 'datum' peg to which all other levels may be referred. Then mark out where the wall is to go using taut string and pegs.

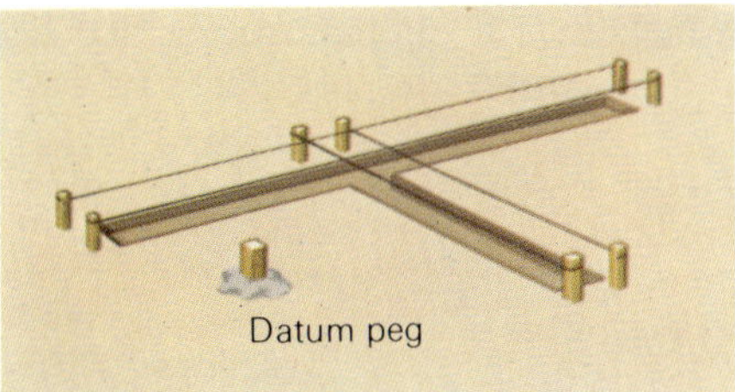

Marking out foundations for a wall with pegs and string. Note separate datum peg.

Foundation

A level and sound concrete foundation is necessary to support the wall, and a trench should be dug about twice to three times as wide as the wall is thick, depending on soil type and height of the wall. Remember to allow extra trench width at the piers. Make the trench about 350 mm (14 in) deep, and perhaps deeper on very heavy clay soils. Concrete will fill the trench to 150 mm (6 in) below ground level. The concrete will thus be 200 mm (8 in) thick. Alternatively, to save expense, you can fill the bottom 75 to 100 mm (3 to 4 in) of the trench with well-rammed hard-core before pouring in the concrete to the level stated. To make sure that the concrete will be of the correct level and depth throughout, incorporate a series of wooden pegs about 1 m (3 ft) apart into the trench

Right top Laying concrete foundation for a low wall. **Right centre** Laying the first course and checking the level. **Right below** Topping the wall with stone coping to protect the bricks.

bottom, using the spirit level and straight edge. The level of the top of the first peg can be referred, if necessary, to the datum peg. Once the level of the first peg has been established, drive in a second one till it is exactly the same height as the first, and so on down the length of the trench.

An alternative to the pegs for use in long trenches is to use a garden hose filled with water and fitted with a 200 mm (8 in) length of clear plastic tube pushed into each end. One end is tied to the side of the first trench peg, and then the furthest peg can be set to the same level as the first by observing the water level in the plastic tubes.

Once these two peg levels are fixed the intermediate pegs can be set using three home-made boning rods, the height of each of which must be the same. At least two people are needed for this job. One holds a boning rod vertically and sights over the T-piece. A second person sets the intermediate rod in line with the other two.

On sloping ground the foundation must be made in a series of steps. Make sure that each step overlaps the one below it by at least 150 mm (6 in) and that the height of the step is equal to that of an exact number of courses of bricks or blocks, including mortar. To hold the foundation concrete at the higher level use a stout piece of board held in position with sturdy pegs.

CONCRETING Full details on the preparation of concrete are given in Chapter 5. A suitable concrete mix consists of Portland cement, sharp sand, and stones of 40 mm ($1\frac{1}{2}$ in) diameter maximum in the proportions 1:3:5 by volume. Ensure that the mix is not too sloppy: it should be on the dry side but just workable. Level and compact the concrete so that the peg tops are flush with the concrete surface. Smooth with the back of the shovel or, better, with a wooden float. Avoid high spots in the finished surface; low spots can be lost in the first layer of mortar. Leave the concrete to harden for at least 5 days.

Brick and block laying

If you have little or no previous experience of bricklaying you would be well advised to practise with some second-hand bricks and very weak mortar, building up a practice corner which can be pulled down afterwards. Ensure that you follow the bonding rules. Work carefully to ensure that all bricks or blocks are laid level and plumb. Prepare mortar of the right consistency, and at all costs keep mortar off the brick/blockwork. Tidy up ('point') the joints afterwards. Keep the wall as dry as possible during building.

BONDING, or staggering of the vertical mortar joints between the bricks, is fundamental to the strength of the wall. Six bonding systems are shown in the drawings on the opposite page. To achieve the bonding effect with 200 to 225 mm (8 to 9 in) thick brickwork a special brick ('queen closer') is needed. This is made by splitting a brick lengthwise with the bolster chisel and lump hammer. One queen closer is usually needed per layer at each corner, or one every other layer for a plain wall end, and it is always placed immediately alongside the corner brick. One advantage of English garden-wall bond is that a queen closer is needed only for the header course.

TECHNIQUES If the wall is to be of precise length (for example, to fit between two buildings), 'run out the bond' by shifting the bricks or blocks along the foundation concrete in order to avoid having to cut any of them. Make stacks of bricks at convenient intervals to reduce the amount of walking once building begins; likewise, have the mortar board within easy reach. It is generally convenient for bricks to be laid damp; play a hosepipe over them the day before use.

Always begin at the wall ends or corners and build to about 600 to 900 mm (2 to 3 ft) high, ensuring that the end-on corner bricks or blocks are carefully checked for level and that the corner is perfectly plumb. The intermediate brickwork between the built-up ends can then be laid by stretching a line for each successive course.

Spread a layer of mortar 500 to 700 mm (20 to 28 in) along the line of the wall. Furrow the top to spread it out, trim the edge of the mortar, and lay a brick. Tap it gently with the handle of the trowel to bed it down: the optimum bed thickness is 10 mm ($\frac{3}{8}$ in). Check the brick for level and plumb, using the spirit level. Butter the end of another brick and lay it up to the first, and repeat the checking procedure. As the bricks are bedded down, excess mortar is squeezed out. This should be trimmed with the trowel on an upward stroke without contaminating the face of the brickwork; the trimmed mortar can now be used to butter the end of the

Split-level concrete foundations. Each level should overlap the one below it by at least one brick length.

Use pegs to mark the correct level of the surface of the concrete foundation.

Brick-bonding systems. Stretcher bond, a simple arrangement with bricks laid lengthwise on each course.

Stretcher bond with integrated pier, the latter integrated into the wall by being laid with alternate headers and stretchers.

English bond, a wall of double thickness in which a course of headers alternates with a course of stretchers.

Queen closer, a brick split in half.

English garden-wall bond: three courses of stretchers followed by one course of headers, the latter using a queen closer.

Flemish bond, in which each course is made up of alternate headers and stretchers, and requires a queen closer at corners.

Flemish wall bond: one header alternating with three stretchers; each course requires a queen closer at corners.

next brick. You lay the blocks in much the same way as bricks, but dry and with a slightly stiffer mortar.

POINTING Nothing spoils the appearance of a wall more than badly finished joints. When pointing is done depends on the individual, but many professionals point the joints just before a batch of mortar is about to run out. By then the mortar is likely to be a little stiffer, and so is easier to point. Gaps in the mortar are made good with mortar applied from the pointing trowel. Once the mortar is 'thumbprint hard' it should be smoothed to give a dense, neat appearance. It is imperative that pointing tools are kept clean and rust free to prevent staining of the mortar.

Keeping the wall dry

The interior of a well-built brick wall remains dry throughout its useful life. This is important because damp bricks not only can suffer severe damage from frost but encourage the growth of algae, especially on north-facing surfaces. Efflorescence, the development of white salts on the face of brickwork, is another annoying feature commonly found in damp walls. What happens is that ground-water salts get carried up into the brickwork in solution, and when the water evaporates the salts are left behind on the surface. They can be brushed off, but may impair the surface texture of the bricks.

Soil moisture, drawn up by capillary action, rather than rain is the chief cause of destructive damp in walls. This moisture can be intercepted by including a damp-proof course near the base of the wall. The commonest form of damp-proof course is made of bitumen felt, of which several proprietary brands are available. Alternatives are to incorporate two layers of engineering bricks in the lowest courses, or two layers of slate bedded in mortar with the joints staggered.

The upper surface of bricks or blocks is generally not capable of weathering well and keeping rainwater out, so that you will need some sort of coping, and ideally another damp-proof course immediately beneath it. For brick walls nothing is better than a layer of the same bricks set on edge, with or without a creasing course. Block walls can be neatly capped with concrete coping 'stones' which should incorporate throating so that drips of water are not able to run down the wall. Ensure that the stones are firmly bedded down on mortar.

Expansion joints

If the wall is greater than about 10 m (33 ft) in length it is highly desirable to incorporate expansion joints at intervals of no more than 9 m (30 ft). This will help to prevent the wall cracking in hot weather. One of the most effective and unobtrusive ways to allow for expansion is to leave a 12 mm ($\frac{1}{2}$ in) vertical gap at the junction with a pier. To prevent daylight showing through, the joint can be staggered. A compressible mastic sealer can be inserted in the gap to keep out water and improve the appearance.

Where one wall joins along the length of another, the partition wall should not be bonded into the main one. A similar expansion joint can be left, and to give strength a greased metal dowel bar is incorporated in the bed of mortar for every fourth brick or every block.

Top Damp-proof courses: a double course of brick tiles, with staggered joints, has been laid beneath the coping at the top of the wall, and bitumen felt inserted between courses nearer ground level. Above A double layer of slate tiles, with staggered joints, also makes a good damp-proof course. Above right Starter bars in the foundation reinforce the lowest course of a hollow-block wall. Steel rods are attached to the bars for higher courses, the hollows being filled with concrete in order to keep the reinforcement rigid.

Reinforcement

This may be necessary if the garden wall is a retaining type, or is high and very exposed to wind, or if gates or doors are to be hung from it. Reinforcement is normally installed vertically, and it is here that hollow concrete blocks have an advantage over solid bricks. Vertical 'starter' bars should be incorporated in the foundation concrete; then steel rod or angle iron is pushed through the hollow blocks and fairly sloppy concrete poured in and well compacted.

Piers for gate posts should always have a stout steel bar or 50 × 50 mm (2 × 2 in) angle iron up the centre. Since it is not so easy to bond in piers in a concrete-block wall, reinforce the mortar bed with expanded metal.

Building aids

A number of wall-building aids are now available which help the amateur to achieve almost professional standards of finish. For instance, you will be able to produce much neater courses if you use special plastic inserts known as brick spacers. Mortar gauges are also an aid to achieving an even bed of mortar, and prevent mortar getting on to the surface of bricks. (However, since bricks and blocks often vary a bit in size, you may need to vary the bed thickness in order to get the courses level.) The Bricklap system consists of a range of concrete bricks with a recess on the top, into which mortar is poured with a special mortar gauge. Since the mortar joints are completely sealed no pointing is necessary.

A plain concrete block wall can be transformed into a 'brick' wall by use of 15 mm ($\frac{5}{8}$ in) thick stick-on brick tiles. The tiles are expensive, however, and would be a considerable extravagance on a large garden wall.

Screen-block walls

Always follow the manufacturers' instructions. Pilasters (vertical strengtheners) built of brick or special slotted-concrete blocks, are needed at intervals of about 3 m (10 ft) if they are not reinforced, but can be placed a little wider apart if they are reinforced with steel rod and concrete. Once you have 'run out the bond' with the screen blocks and located the exact position of the pilasters, you can begin building them up, ensuring that they are exactly level and upright.

Stretch a line in between the partially constructed pilasters and begin laying the screen blocks. Make sure that you keep an even 10 to 12 mm ($\frac{3}{8}$ to $\frac{1}{2}$ in) joint of mortar and take care not to get the mortar on to the exposed face of the blocks. Of course, no bonding effect is possible with this type of wall, but its strength can be increased by incorporating strips of expanded metal or small-mesh wire netting in the mortar bed. For safety reasons you should not build the wall more than six blocks high. It should be finished off with coping, and the tops of the pilasters should be capped.

Pierced screen blocks with special pilasters make an attractive wall.

Building a pierced-screen-block wall: slotting in a first-course pilaster.

The mortar joint between each of the blocks is strengthened with strips of wire mesh.

Checking the level. Walls of this type should not be more than six blocks high.

Building stone walls

The building of a handsome stone wall needs a good deal of skill and patience in the selection and fitting together of the stones. The finished wall should present a pleasing pattern of stones nicely integrated into a unified whole. Whether or not mortar is used, keep the following points in mind:

Try to bond the stones.

Use a greater proportion of larger stones in the lower layers and smaller stones in the upper layers.

Avoid placing stones of the same shape and size next to each other.

If using mortar, do not overdo it. Select stones to keep the mortar bed thin: they should not appear to be emerging from a pulpy mass.

Build the wall to a *batter* (wider at the base than at the top). The wall should narrow by 30 to 40 mm ($1\frac{1}{4}$ to $1\frac{3}{4}$ in) for each 300 mm (12 in) of height.

The traditional dry-stone walls in hill country usually have no concrete foundation, but if you intend to use mortar you should lay a conventional strip foundation as for a brick or block wall. On gradually sloping ground the wall follows the ground contour, so a

A wall made of reconstituted stone often achieves a natural-looking effect.

stepped foundation is needed only for a steep slope. Arrange the stone in piles of assorted shapes and sizes along the length of the trench to reduce the amount of walking you have to do once building is in progress. Before mixing up the mortar, experiment by arranging a group of stones so that they form an interesting, closely locking pattern. To achieve a fairly regular surface on both sides it is usually best to construct the wall of two leaves (double thickness), with the occasional bonding stone going right through the wall for extra strength. Do not hesitate to knock corners off awkwardly shaped stones for the sake of producing a tight fit. Use a fairly stiff mortar mix, filling in all the joints thoroughly. Small offcut pieces of stone should be included in the centre of the wall between the two leaves to make it really solid.

Once a section of the wall has been laid and the mortar has begun to harden a little, a good profile effect is achieved if the joints are raked out with a blunt stick so that the stones stand about 15 mm ($\frac{5}{8}$in) proud of the mortar.

Build up the ends just as you would a brick or block wall, and try to keep the batter uniform. Rather than rely on the eye for doing this you can use a home-made two-piece setting frame, with one piece to represent the vertical and the other attached to it at the desired angle of batter. Once the ends are built up, lines can be stretched along each side of the wall and the centre section can then be completed. For the top of the wall try to select fairly flat stones that will level out irregularities.

Dry-stone walls

This is generally no job for the amateur. Considerable skill and experience is needed, particularly in 'dressing' the stone to produce a wall that is safe and strong. One of the essential features of such structures is the large, flat 'band stones' going right through the wall.

An additional attraction of dry-stone walling is that it enables you to incorporate plants within the wall. Plants are most likely to thrive if the centre of the wall is filled up with soil into which the roots are well bedded.

Right above Proprietary-stone retaining wall with stone coping. **Right below** Wall and raised bed made from multiple 'bricks' of proprietary stone.

Special features

Archways

The construction of a brick archway needs some care and a certain amount of patience. It is usual to construct a semi-circular arch in which the bricks are wedged into position. To hold the bricks in place during construction you will need to make a sturdy timber template; a frame made from wood of 100 × 50 mm (4 × 2 in) section fitted with a semi-circular 'skin' of 3 mm ($\frac{1}{8}$ in) plywood makes a satisfactory template.

In forming the arch you can lay the bricks with either the header faces or the stretcher faces showing. If the arch is formed with stretcher faces showing you will have to accept wide and rather ugly mortar joints between the tops of the faces, or you will need to cut the bricks into wedge shapes – a tricky job for the inexperienced. On the whole, then, an arch with header faces showing is a better bet for the amateur builder. If extra strength is needed, two courses of heading bricks can be formed. Alternatively you can use perforated bricks threaded onto two 6 mm ($\frac{1}{4}$ in) steel bars bent into semi-circles.

Top Plywood template used in construction of a header-face brick arch. **Opposite page** Doorway with double-header arch.

Details of the structure of an arch template. The supporting legs must rest on firm ground.

Brickwork patterns

These can be incorporated into the surface of a long plain wall to create interest. All kinds of wall sculpture can be formed, but do not be too ambitious in your early efforts – you may impair the strength of the wall.

Curving walls

A curving, or serpentine, brick wall is not only stronger than a straight one but it can be graceful in appearance and help detract from the angularity of most suburban gardens. The most important point is to ensure that the curve, or curves, are pleasing to the eye and, in particular, that a succession of curves joins smoothly and blends together.

Particular care is needed in marking out. Draw a plan on paper first, using compasses, and then transfer the plan to the ground, using a peg the correct distance from the wall, a piece of string, and a cane to scratch the appropriate arc into the soil. Avoid making the radii too tight – it will generally mean that the vertical mortar joints are unattractively wide on the outside of the curve.

Once the foundation concrete has hardened mark out the exact line of the wall with chalk and begin building. No builder's lines can be used, so you have a choice of using the spirit level and your eye, or you can make a wooden template made from 75 × 25 mm (3 × 1 in) framing fitted with a skin of 3mm ($\frac{1}{8}$ in) thick hardboard that you have shaped to the curve required.

Circular piers or seats

A low curving wall terminating in a low circular pedestal can be an attractive innovation, and it need not be too difficult to construct. The bricks will have to be tapered by cutting them with the bolster chisel, but by using a heading bond any poorly cut surfaces will be hidden. The wall centre can be filled with rubble and concrete, but the top layer of bricks must be carefully cut and fitted together.

Right above Low walls can be given a 'rustic' effect by using a variety of building materials. Awkwardly shaped pieces, however, may result in unattractive mortar joints.
Right below A curving wall relieves the angularity of garden lines. Before building, mark out the arc on the ground with a peg, string, and cane.

Wall recesses

Another source of interest is the variety of ledges that can be formed in walls to accommodate plant pots or troughs. Recessed ledges must have a proper lintel in the form of either a curved arch (as described above) or a flat arch in which the brick or block-work is held in position by, for instance, a length of 50 × 50 mm (2 × 2 in) section angle iron. The ledge should slope very slightly forward so that it throws water away from the wall back.

Wall creepers

The appearance of a large expanse of wall can often be enhanced with a creeper. Some of these plants are self attaching, but the majority need some form of framework to cling to. One of the most unobtrusive can be produced by a criss-cross series of galvanised steel wires spaced regularly over the wall surface. Drill and plug holes in the appropriate positions in the mortar joints, and be sure to use stainless steel, galvanised, or black-painted screws to avoid rust marks staining the wall.

An alternative method is to use wooden trellis or plastic mesh. Both types need to be fixed so that there is a gap between wall and trellis. Cotton reels sawn in half can be used as spacers, but a better solution is to screw 50 × 25 mm (2 × 1 in) section timber uprights to the wall, and then fix the trellis or netting to the uprights with galvanised nails.

Above A dry-stone wall with recesses for plants. **Right** A simple trellis attached to a brick wall offers support for this clematis.

3 Fences and Gates

GENERALLY speaking a garden fence is significantly cheaper than a wall. On the other hand, it requires more maintenance, has inferior sound-deadening properties, and will not last as long as a well-built wall. Its shorter life-span, however, is not necessarily a disadvantage. Many people, for instance, prefer a natural barrier such as a hedge and use a fence to provide a measure of privacy until the hedge plantings have reached maturity. Whether permanent or temporary, fences are available in a wide variety of sizes and forms, are comparatively easy to erect, and – in many cases – can later be dismantled for use elsewhere in the garden.

A fence can serve the function of marking one's boundary or providing a simple form of partitioning within the garden. The more substantial types can give a high degree of security, denying entry to people, animals, and even airborne objects such as footballs. But however much you value your privacy, you should consider carefully before erecting a tall, solid fence around a small garden. It can not only make the garden appear smaller than it really is, but can promote feelings of isolation and claustrophobia. With a little thought, and by using, for instance, a louvre design, privacy can be achieved with interesting shadow effects.

Exposure to wind can not only make growing difficult but also reduces the opportunities for achieving full enjoyment of one's garden. A good, solid fence can provide shelter for both you and your plants. Bear in mind, however, that on very exposed sites a flat-sided, impenetrable fence will be severely tested by high winds and may require extra-firm support. Moreover, a high fence may cause considerable air turbulence – the vertical swirling motion of air on the lee side of an obstruction – which can do quite a lot of damage to prize blooms. Conversely, in very still air conditions, mildew may become a problem in the vicinity of an impenetrable fence. In both such cases the answer may be to use some form of slatted fence which, if carefully designed, can still provide the necessary privacy.

Remember that the shelter provided by a fence (or by a wall) may also shade plants from the sun. If this is likely to be a serious problem a more open fence may be needed. The fence can, in fact, extend the range of plants which can be grown, and can enhance the effect of some: certain plants that fail to compete for attention in the shrub border can look very attractive against a fence panel.

The appearance of the fence should ideally complement that of the plant life in the garden. In particular, you should be careful regarding its colour: any departure from conventional creosote brown, or white for small partitioning fences, will need to be done with taste if the appearance is not to jar.

Likewise, consider design details which might draw the eye to the fence rather than to the plants in the foreground. The outline and surface of the fence should be as regular as possible; the appearance of even the most handsome wooden fence, for instance, can be marred by the use of man-made materials, such as concrete posts.

Ensure that the fence blends with the adjacent plant schemes. A modern ranch-type fence, for example, might look incongruous as a backdrop to the tumbling informality of a rock garden. On the other hand, plants can play an important part in softening the rather austere lines of a boundary fence, and one way of achieving this is to plant so that portions of the fence are concealed behind an area of lush growth.

Fence types

Timber is the material most commonly employed for the construction of garden fences, although one does occasionally come across concrete, rigid plastic, and the more utilitarian wire fences; metal railings, these days, are usually too expensive to consider.

Timber fences

The choice is between solid types – interwoven, lap, and close-boarded forms – and open types such as post-and-rail, slat, louvre, or trellis forms.

SOLID TYPES Interwoven fences consist of panels of wooden slats, usually of larch, secured in a framework fixed between posts. This type is popular and relatively inexpensive, although it is not perhaps as robust as other forms. The standard panel length is 1.8 m (6 ft) and heights are from 900 mm (3 ft) to 1.8 m (6 ft); 'peep proof' forms are

A lap fence offers privacy and shelter.

Post-and-rail

Post-and-rail

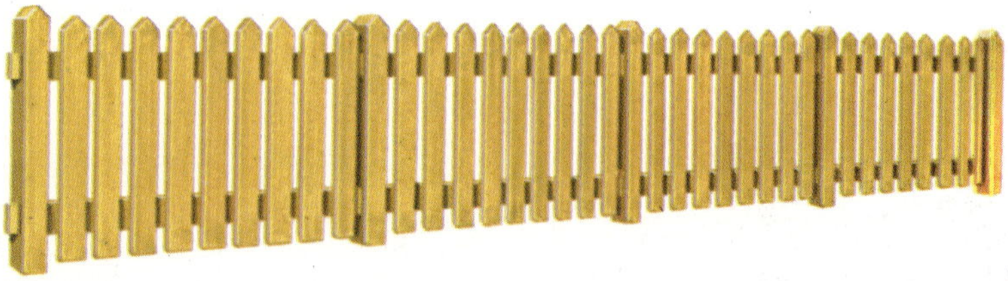

Picket

Interwoven, with trellis top

Lap

Feather edge

available. Lap fencing is made in the same basic sizes, and is a little stronger because it uses thicker overlapping slats; often the edges of the slats have a wavy edge to give a rustic effect. Close-boarded fencing uses feather-edge boarding overlapped usually in the vertical plane. The boards are nailed to two, sometimes three, triangular-section arris rails fitted into slots cut in the fence posts. Alternatively, the slats overlap horizontally and are attached to a frame fixed to the posts. Posts should be spaced not more than 3 m (10 ft) apart. Commonly, there is a gravel board at the base as a protection against intruding animals.

OPEN TYPES One of the commonest forms is the post-and-rail fence. This is simple and fairly inexpensive fencing in which wide horizontal rails are nailed to posts. The number and width of rails are variable, depending on fence height and purposes. The popular ranch style uses two or three wide rails, but taller versions are used, too. Proprietary ranch fencing is available in both rigid-plastic and concrete forms. By fixing rails alternately on front and rear sides of the posts, a permeable yet private barrier is achieved. Palisade fences are among the simplest to make and maintain. The pales are commonly 60 to 75 mm ($2\frac{1}{2}$ to 3 in) wide and 20 mm ($\frac{3}{4}$ in) thick, with spacing between them equal to or a little less than the paling width. The paling tops are usually pointed, although various ornate shapes are found, too. The arris rails used are 75×38 mm ($3 \times 1\frac{1}{2}$ in) in section and are slotted into 100×100 mm (4×4 in) posts at not more than 3 m (10 ft) intervals. The slat type is a popular alternative to the palisade fence. Usually, 50×25 mm (2×1 in) slats set 12 to 25 mm ($\frac{1}{2}$ to 1 in) apart, are nailed to arris rails located at top and bottom. An alternative form has every second slat nailed to the other side of the rails, giving a greater degree of privacy. Louvres, which are set at right angles to the area of privacy, need boards strong enough to resist warping; they are usually 38 mm ($1\frac{1}{2}$ in) thick and 125 mm (5 in) wide. The trellis fence is suitable only as a lightweight screen in a sheltered position.

Typical open and solid fences; the latter are available as proprietary packs.

OTHER TYPES Various forms of wire fence are sometimes used around the garden – the best known being the chain link. Avoid the galvanised form: once the zinc coating wears off it rusts and looks hideous. Plastic-coated forms are preferable, if hardly picturesque. Although it offers no privacy, this form of fencing is quite impenetrable to animals. Plastic-coated wire hoops are available as border fencing for setting off path edges and the like, and act as a deterrent to walking on the grass.

Buying fencing

Most forms of timber fencing are available as made up panels, although costs can be trimmed by buying a packaged fence kit. In such a kit all the components for each panel are supplied precut, and with the aid of only a hammer you assemble the panels on site as the fence is erected. Less expensive still – although not cheap, owing to the price of any timber nowadays – is to design and build your own fence, using standard timber sizes.

If you decide to do this, remember two golden rules: first, do not skimp on the size and spacing of the frames and posts; second, always use seasoned and treated timber.

Fence posts

These are the most critical components because they govern the strength and longevity of the fence, and usually they are the first part to give trouble. Timber, plastic, and concrete posts can be used. The latter two have the advantage that they are not subject to rotting; but most people find them less attractive than timber. As far as timber posts are concerned, oak is the most durable but it is very expensive; the best alternative is treated larch. Preservation is of the utmost importance: use either pressure- or vacuum-treated timber or posts that have been steeped in, rather than merely painted with, creosote. Information about preserving timber is given in Chapter 8.

For solid fencing the normal size of post to use is 75 × 75 mm (3 × 3 in) section, although 50 × 75 mm (2 × 3 in) section is sometimes used; for open fencing 100 × 100 mm (4 × 4 in) is the norm. The post length, for solid-panel fencing, is usually about 600 mm (2 ft) longer than the fence height, allowing it to be set about 550 mm (22 in) in the ground while still overtopping the panels by about 50 mm (2 in). Longer posts may be needed if the ground is loose or falls away on one side and also for fences greater than 1.5 m (5 ft) in height.

A fairly recent innovation is a post support consisting of a steel spike driven into the ground and incorporating a 75 × 75 mm (3 × 3 in) holder in which the post can be fixed just above ground level. The saving in post length partly offsets the cost of the supports, but the main advantage is that the posts are less liable to rot because they are not in direct contact with the soil. Moreover, such supports sometimes make it possible to re-use old posts that have rotted away at ground level. It is vital to drive the spikes absolutely vertically into the ground and to correct any twisting before the spike is fully home.

The tops of the timber posts should be protected against rain soaking into the grain. You can cut the post top off at an angle, so it will shed water; but a neater effect is often achieved by using caps which overlap the top by about 20 mm (¾ in) all round.

Erecting fences

It is wise to choose a day when the weather is not only dry but calm: wind-blown panels or planking make for bad fences and worse tempers. You will need a line, spirit level, hammer, nails, and a spade or a post-hole borer. This last item works somewhat like a corkscrew and can be bought or hired from the fence supplier. The particular value of such a tool is that less soil is disturbed than when a hole is dug with a spade, and generally the hole can be made much quicker. If you live in the country, you may be lucky enough to borrow a tractor-operated post-hole digger from a friendly farmer.

Mark the exact line of the fence using the line and 2 stakes, and then lay out the posts at the approximate spacings. Dig or bore the first hole 150 mm (6 in) deeper than required and fill in the extra depth with rubble or stones well rammed down. This will help to drain water away from the post base. Put the post in position and check that it is the correct height. Ram about 200 mm (8 in) of earth into the hole, and use the spirit level to get the post plumb upright. Continue filling the hole with small amounts of soil, ramming it down with a small piece of timber; the more thoroughly that this is done the more firmly will the post be fixed. Alternate fillings of soil and finely broken hardcore will help to achieve an even firmer fixing. Check that the post is upright after each filling has been rammed down. On loose soils, or if the fence is over 1.5 m (5 ft) high, or is exposed to strong winds, a firmer fixing is achieved by attaching a wooden cleat to the post bottom, or by filling the top half of the hole with concrete. Use a dryish mix and ram it well round the post. Slope the top of the concrete so that it will throw water away from the post.

Erecting panel fences

Once the first post is firm and plumb, stretch a taut piece of string between the top of it and a stake set in at the far end of the fence. The string should indicate the exact height of the panel tops. Use a panel to mark the position of the next post hole, and dig or bore it out. It is more convenient to do this now than when the panel is in position. Rest the panels on bricks or timber to keep it about 50 mm (2 in) clear of the ground (this will prevent it rotting) then butt it up to the centre of the side of the first post. Attach the panel (on both sides) with galvanized nails long enough to penetrate at least half way into the post. Now set the second post into its hole, bringing it into firm contact with the other edge of the panel. Check both post and panel for plumb and level, and ram earth and hardcore into the hole.

Proceed in this way, ensuring that the panel tops are exactly located along the guideline, which must be kept really taut. As a further check, I generally find it useful also to sight along the fence line as each panel is being nailed into position.

On sloping ground it will be necessary to step the panels. If the slope is a gradual one do not use a tiny step for each panel: it looks better if you make a bolder, 100 to 150 mm (4 to 6 in) step every two or three panels. Remember that at each of these points you will need a post whose length is greater by the amount of the step.

If the ground is higher on one side of the fence by no more than about 250 mm (10 in), a small soil-retaining structure of 50 mm (2 in) paving slabs set in concrete should be placed on the higher side. For steeper slopes you will have to build a proper brick or block retaining wall (*see* Chapter 4).

Finish the fence off with capping for the panels and posts; pre-drill the post caps to avoid splitting them.

Erecting other types

The general technique for erecting the posts is as already described. Then proceed as follows.

RANCH FENCING is quite simple to construct by nailing, or preferably screwing, 125 × 25 mm (5 × 1 in) boards to 100 × 100 mm (4 × 4 in) posts. The neat appearance of such fences depends greatly on the boards having close-fitting vertical butt joints.

PALISADE AND CLOSE-BOARDED FENCES The sequence of construction is, first, to mortise the posts. After the first post has been erected and while the second is being positioned in its hole, slot the arris rails into the mortises of both posts; then firm in the second post. As with all other fencing, check constantly that the posts are being erected plumb upright. Once all the posts and rails are in position the pales or cladding can be attached.

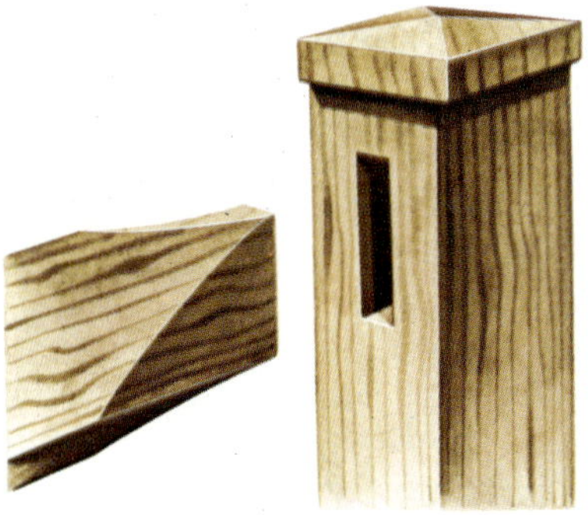

Rail-end cut to fit into a post mortise.

Fitting a fence panel: check frequently for vertical and horizontal levels.

Maintenance and repair

Once they have been erected fences tend to be neglected. The most important maintenance work is taking steps to keep rot at bay, which will entail either applying creosote every two years or so or painting. Creosote should be applied only to a dry fence, and remember that plants can be damaged if they come into contact with it. Apply liberal coats and pay particular attention to the post bases. It is worth digging out 200 to 250 mm (8 to 9 in) of soil and soaking the post base thoroughly with creosote, perhaps pouring some around the post.

Painting of fences is best done after a prolonged period of dry weather, which is why it is usually done in the autumn. Scrape and burn off loose paint and remove all traces of dirt and algae. Prime bare patches and use good quality undercoat and gloss top coat suitable for outdoor use.

After the winter's high winds some posts may become loosened, and they should be re-firmed by digging out about 300 mm (12 in) of soil and ramming it back.

Check for rotting gravel boards and posts. It is obviously preferable to replace them at a time convenient to you rather than when you are compelled to do so as a result of the ravages of a gale. Moreover, an entire fence can be seriously damaged as a result of a single rotting post breaking off in a gale.

There are a number of ways in which a post can be replaced. If the timber above ground level is sound the post can be sawn off at the highest convenient point, and a spur post set in concrete alongside. Extend the spur post at least 30 cm (12 in) up the old one and fix with two bolts or coach-screws. Angle the top of the spur to throw water off.

The alternative might be to use one of the proprietary spiked post holders. The post will probably need to be detached from the fence panels to facilitate this. Prise the nailed framework from the post, taking care not to split it. If necessary drill the nail heads in order to remove them. Once the framework has been prised away by about 6 mm ($\frac{1}{4}$ in) or so it is usually possible to cut the nail with a hacksaw. Dig out the old post base and fix the replacement post, ensuring that it is well preserved and upright.

Occasionally gale damage results in a portion of the fence blowing down as a result of rotted posts. You will then be faced not only with post replacement but also re-assembly of panels which have been pulled apart from the framework. In the case of solid panels collect all the pieces and carefully re-assemble them into the framework, using a flat surface, such as a garage floor, as a base.

When open-type fences are blown down, it often happens that the rails remain sound except for splits developing around the nail holes. It is usually a

1

2

3

Above Fence and gate posts must be firmly mounted. Cleats (1) and concrete (2) both provide extra stability below ground level. A spur post (3) either of concrete, as here, or of timber can be used to repair a post that has rotted at or near ground level.

simple matter to drill new holes, but remember to plug the splits with putty.

If arris rails have to be replaced, you may find that they will not fit into both mortises. To save yourself the trouble of removing one of the posts, set one end of the rail into one of the mortises and the other end (which may need to be shortened slightly) into a mortise-shaped slot cut in a piece of timber. This piece can then be nailed on to the side of the other post. Alternatively, the arris rail can be cut into two using a long diagonal cut (scarf joint); after the ends of the rail have been fitted into the mortised posts, the joint can be glued and screwed together.

Gates

Gates are made of timber or metal and are available in a wide range of styles and sizes. The gate to one's property is often the first garden feature to be noticed by the visitor or passer-by. It is likely to give an impression of your taste and even of your character in general – so it is worth giving the question of choice a good deal of thought. At all events, the entrance gate will be in constant use, so it should be durable, attractive, and easily operated.

The style should be chosen with great care to blend with the architectural tone of your home and the character of your garden. If the garden is bounded by wooden fencing, it is sensible to select a gate which is made of the same material and which is of a similar or at least a compatible design. Otherwise, choose a design which both harmonises with the surroundings – gates in town tend to be more formal than those in rural areas – and complements the character of the garden within and the scale of your property; nothing looks more pretentious, for

Below The main elements in the construction of a typical garden gate.

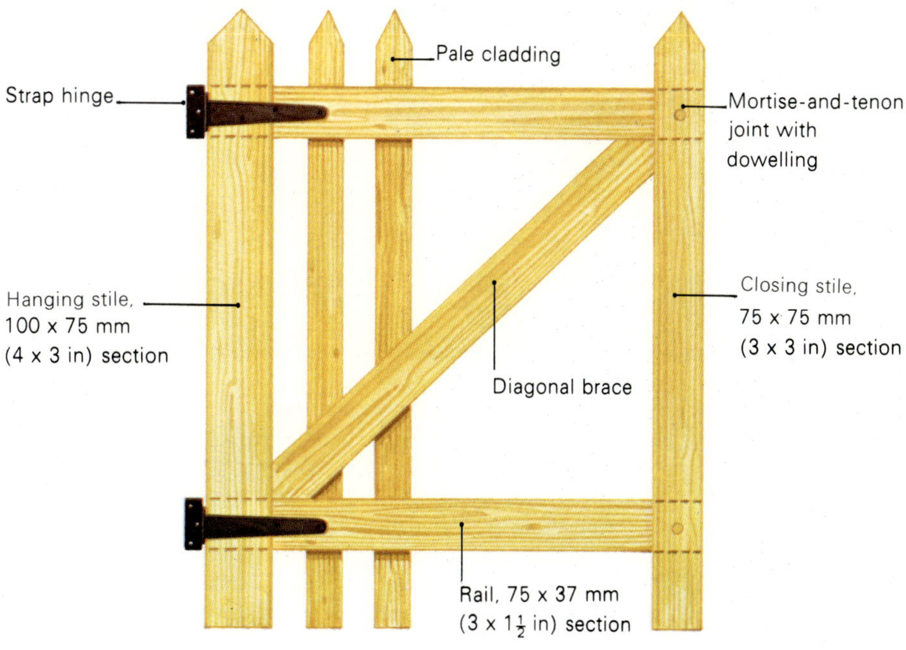

instance, than massive wrought-iron gates giving access to a modest suburban semi-detached. Finally, of course, your choice of design will be influenced by price and by various practical considerations – for instance, whether the gate needs to keep pets and children in (or out).

Posts

Gate posts should be sturdy and should complement the design of the gate itself: with a wall it is more appropriate to build reinforced piers rather than use posts; with fences or hedges, timber or concrete posts will be needed. The appearance of concrete posts can be improved if they are painted with cement-based paint in a colour to match the gate. Concrete posts can either be bought or made at home. They must be reinforced with steel bars but, unlike wood, they are not prone to rot.

Appropriate timber posts are oak, which is the most durable but is not suitable for painting, or pressure-impregnated softwood, which is cheaper and can be painted. It is important to remember that the hanging post should be both wide enough and installed deep enough to take the pull of the gate. For this reason, with a drive gate the hanging post will need to be about 175 × 175 mm (7 × 7 in) in cross section and should be set at least 900 mm (3 ft) in the ground; the other post can be 125 × 125 mm (5 × 5 in). The post for pedestrian gates is usually 100 × 100 mm (4 × 4 in) in cross section.

Make sure that the posts are perfectly upright and are made rigid by frequent ramming of the infill.

Below Drive gates need a substantial hanging post to prevent sagging. **Right below** Typical gate hinges.

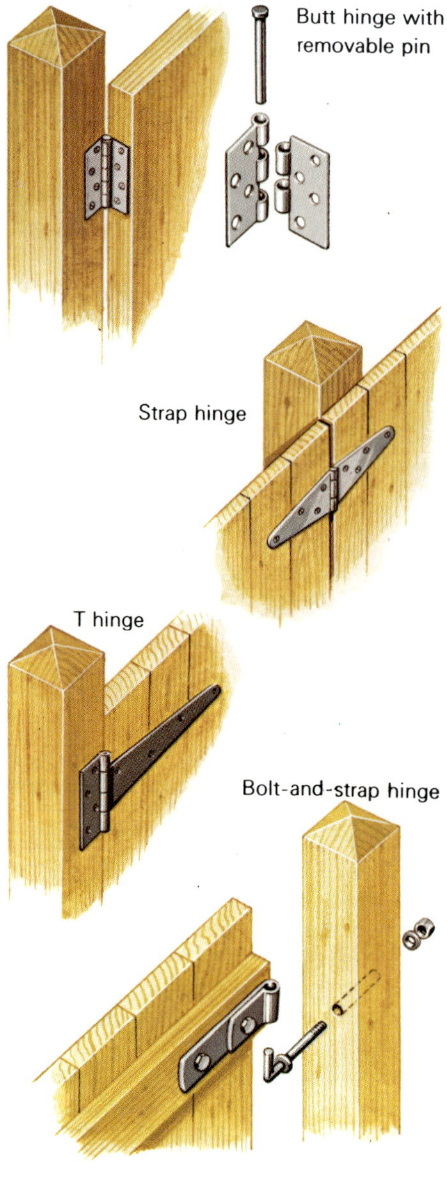

Construction

Ensure that the timber you buy is not warped, and that it is well seasoned; if possible let it dry out for a week or so before use. A gate is made up of two sturdy stiles (the outer uprights), rails (the cross-pieces), bracing (usually diagonal pieces to help prevent sagging), and possibly cladding (boards, slats, or whatever to give it a solid, continuous surface). For strength and to avoid water entering the joints, try to construct the gate as far as possible using mortise-and-tenon joints pinned with wooden dowelling. For a five-bar gate nails need be used only for the bracing. Note that the diagonal brace can act only by pushing at the end liable to sag, so that it should run from the lower hinged corner to the upper gate-catch corner.

Before the posts are fixed the appropriate gate fitting should be selected; these will determine the spacing between the posts. Apart from their use with very light gates it is best to avoid butt hinges and to select strap hinges,

The life of timber gates and fences can be greatly extended if they are regularly repainted or treated with preservative.

one form of which enables the gate to be detached from the posts quite readily. Larger, single-drive gates will need hook-and-ride hinges. Spring-loaded self-closing hinges can be an advantage if you have young children. If the gates are to be hung from brick piers, special hook hinges are available for bedding into the mortar joint.

There is a wide choice of catches, of which the auto-catch type is the most convenient, while the ring-catch type is perhaps the most attractive. Double-drive gates can either be secured with a metal loop that can be lifted over the stile on the other gate; or, more conveniently, one of the gates can be fitted with a drop bolt and the other with a latch.

Having selected the desired hinge and catch arrangement, fix the posts into position with, for a typical garden gate, an extra 10 to 15 mm ($\frac{3}{8}$ to $\frac{5}{8}$ in) between the posts to prevent binding, particularly at the closing end; ensure that the posts are upright and firm. Then lift the gate temporarily into position and mark the location of the hinges and catches; these should then be fixed with the longest possible screws. There may be a certain amount of 'play' in the hinges. This must be taken up at once or the gate will soon begin to sag.

Maintenance

It is very annoying to have to grapple with a gate that will not open or close easily. The usual troubles are that the gate sags, or binds, or will not latch.

A heavy gate is almost certain eventually to cause a minor movement of the hanging post – the amount depending on how firmly the post was fixed in the first place. If there is an appreciable amount of sag it may be necessary to refix the post. Otherwise sagging can result from worn, broken, or partly detached hinges. If the screws have come out, the holes can be plugged and/or longer screws used.

Binding may, of course, be a result of the gate sagging; if it is not, plane a little wood off the closing stile. Detached latches can be replaced in a similar way to detached hinges.

Always discourage children from swinging on gates, and remove objects that may interfere with them opening properly. Oil the hinges every few months. Check the gates every year or so for any rotted timbers and replace them as necessary. Paint or apply preservative to softwood gates regularly to ensure a long and attractive life.

4 Beds, Borders, and Retaining Walls

With the boundaries of the property properly enclosed you can now set about marking out the areas intended for plants and for the lawn. In order to stagger the workload and the capital outlay some people prefer to get the general topography perfectly right and only to grass down all the non-hard-surfaced areas in the first season. This has several advantages: you can extend the period for planning and get it right; you can form bed edges more easily because you will be cutting them from an established lawn; and you can be sure that your plants get off to a good start by planting out each of them at the correct time. On the other hand, most people prefer to plant up at the outset to get the garden established as soon as possible.

Before doing any marking out on site, plan the layout carefully on a large piece of paper. It is a good idea to rough out several alternative schemes, eventually combining the best features of each to arrive at a scheme that is attractive, efficient in its use of space, and easy to maintain. You will almost certainly find this paperwork to have been well worth while: it is much easier to wield a rubber eraser than to move established plants, lawn, paving stones, or garden shed.

Beds and borders

To improve a long thin garden, beds can be best arranged crosswise rather than lengthwise; curving beds and borders can often help to ameliorate the angularity of the typical garden site.

When subdividing the garden area and creating interesting shapes, try to keep to a minimum the number of small pieces of lawn isolated by flower beds; they will be a tiresome chore to mow. You can break up a grassed area, and still have continuity for mowing, by snaking the layout, and creating

beds which partially cut off adjacent areas of lawn. Very acute angles of lawn are generally best avoided for they, too, can make mowing difficult into the points. Remember that the more ornate the chosen shapes of bed, the greater will be the length of lawn edges which must be trimmed; it is here that a powered lawn-edge trimmer can be a great asset.

Finally, the depth of borders should be considered, within the site constraints, in terms of impact and convenience. A deep bed carefully packed with a succession of tiered blooms can be a great attraction – but it can be very inconvenient from a weeding point of view, particularly when the soil is wet.

Marking out

You will need pegs, canes, stout string that will not stretch easily, a hammer, and a tape; if you have made a builder's square (*see* Chapter 2), this will be useful, too.

Rectangles are fairly easily marked out. One side of the rectangle is often the garden boundary or a path. Mark this first side with pegs and a line, and from the corners take right angles, using the builder's square. Another method of making a right angle is by means of a triangle, as follows. Measure 2 m ($6\frac{1}{2}$ ft) from the corner peg along the first side of the rectangle, and drive in another peg. Attach to this a piece of string and make a knot 2.5 m ($8\frac{1}{4}$ ft) along it from the peg. Likewise attach a piece of string to the corner peg and make a knot 1.5 m (5 ft) from it. Pull the two strings taut, and where the two knots align drive in a third peg. This will give you a line at right angles to the first.

For longer beds it is more accurate if multiples of the basic 1.5, 2, and 2.5 m units are used; alternatively, an 'imperial' triangle can be used based on

Above left A brick raised bed. **Right** A ground plan enables you to integrate beds, borders, and other features.

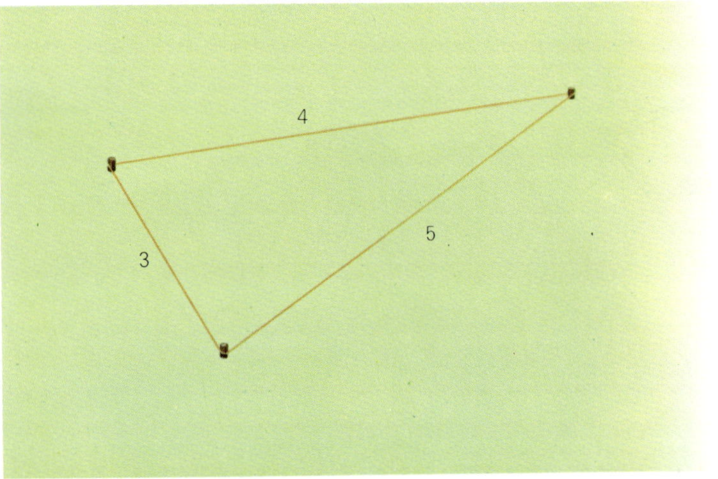

A right-angled triangle of string and pegs or of timber can be made up from sides in units of 3, 4, and 5.

sides of 3, 4, and 5 ft. Once all the corner pegs have been fixed, check the accuracy of the right angles by measuring the diagonals: they should be equal.

Regular curves (arcs) or complete circles are achieved by scratching in the soil with a cane on the end of a line fixed to a peg driven into the ground. To make an oval, begin by pegging out two lines, (AB and CD in diagram) bisecting each other exactly at right-angles, to mark the extreme length and width of the oval. To one of the pegs (A) marking the extreme width, attach a line half as long as the extreme length of the oval, and mark with pegs the two points at which its arc crosses the longest line. Call these two pegs E and F. Now measure the distance from peg E to peg D. Take a piece of string of a length equal to twice that distance and form it into a loop. Place the loop around pegs E and F and, keeping it taut with a cane, you can scratch the outline of an oval in the soil. The size of the oval will depend, of course, on the length of your original bisecting lines. An enormous variety of other geometrical shapes can be formed simply by drawing overlapping arcs, with pegs, line, and cane, from the corners or sides of a square.

It is not usually possible to mark out free shapes geometrically. Rather they must be drawn free hand on the ground by marking with pegs, canes, or a dribble of sand or lime. Often geometric shapes can be used as a basis on which you can extemporize. If you are not satisfied with the shape which you produce, you merely rub out the mark and start again.

As an aid to duplicating a free shape quickly and accurately, you may find it convenient to form a rectangle around it and take a number of key measurements from one of the corners. You can then transfer these measurements into other rectangles that mark the sites where similar free shapes will be drawn. Obviously, with free shapes anything goes, but it is sensible to keep them fairly bold and simple, otherwise they will be hard to duplicate and will look fussy rather than interesting.

Raised beds

Raised beds, although not a common feature of modern gardens, offer the advantages of adding some vertical interest, a degree of variety, and the opportunity of neatly integrating a patio, say, into the general garden plan. They have sound practical advantages, too, in that plants can be grown at a level at which you can tend them without stooping; this makes them especially attractive for elderly or infirm gardeners. However, plants in an isolated growing medium do demand

Marking out an oval (see text). In sketch 1, line AE is half length of CD. In sketch 2, the loop of string is twice the length of ED. String is placed around pegs at E and F, then drawn tight by cane, which can then inscribe the oval through A, B, C, and D.

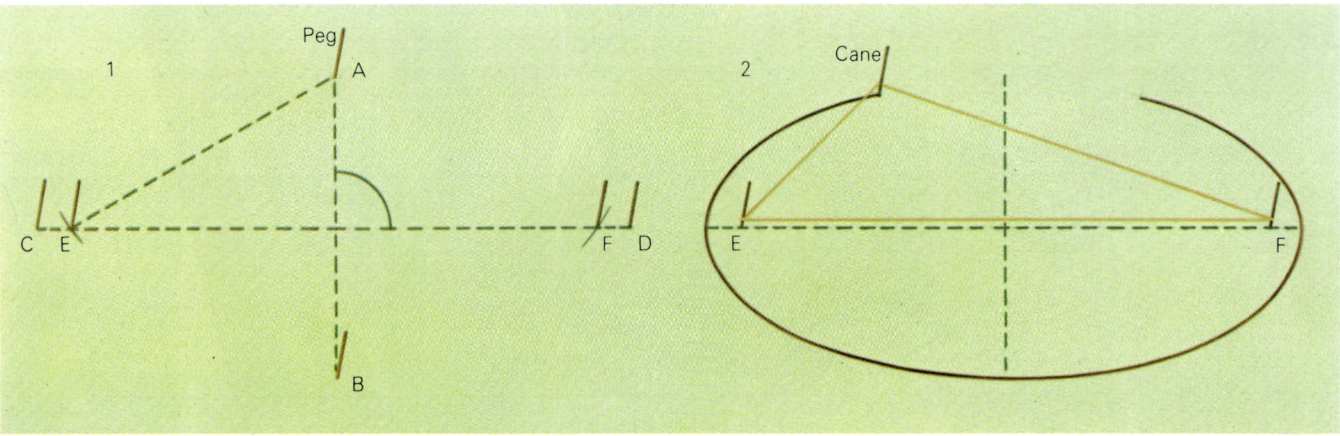

more attention – especially with regard to watering in dry weather – otherwise they will quickly succumb. Drainage is also vitally important to avoid waterlogging in extended wet periods.

Sizes and shapes

The size chosen will of course depend upon the location, but three basic factors should be borne in mind. First, it should not be built so high that the plants cannot be seen effectively by people sitting in the garden. It should not be too small, particularly in width, otherwise the soil will dry out rapidly and will be quickly exhausted by the plants. Most important of all, the height should be convenient for working the bed. The Disabled Living Foundation recommends that the most suitable height for a person working from a wheelchair is 600 mm (2 ft), and for a walking disabled person 850 mm (2 ft 10 in). For such people the bed should not be more than 1.2 m (4 ft) wide.

However, many gardeners feel that aesthetically 450 mm (18 in) is the right height for a raised bed if it is not to dominate a small garden. Thus a walled enclosure about 450 to 800 mm (1 ft 6 in to 2 ft 8 in) high, and with a minimum width of 450 mm (18 in) is a reasonable basis on which owners of small to medium sized gardens can make their calculations.

The most straightforward shape is rectangular. However, if the bed is of a fair size this shape will tend to emphasize, rather than mitigate, the angularity of most gardens. With a little imagination and care in design, a variety of shapes can be developed that will create interest and a sense of style in the garden landscape.

Materials

A wide variety of materials can be used including brick, stone, blocks, mass concrete, pre-cast concrete slabs, peat blocks, rustic timber, and even old railway sleepers. The choice should fall on the material that will harmonise best with the setting: rustic timber or railway sleepers, for instance, would look out of place in the middle of a formal modern patio. If you are thinking of using bricks, consider the possibility of getting hold of some good-quality, nicely mellowed, second-hand samples.

Narrow raised beds can be used to create partitions in the smaller garden. The structural materials are, from left, brick, peat, and dry stone.

If built of stone, raised beds and (as here) retaining walls should be built to a batter, leaning into the higher level.

Construction

Whatever the material used, the bed must be strong enough to withstand the considerable pressure of the soil. If the materials are laid dry it will be worthwhile building to a batter – angling the wall inwards from the vertical.

If bricks or blocks are used it is desirable that they should be given some protection against staining by efflorescence (see page 22). With soil directly in contact with the bricks or blocks, soluble salts are bound to seep through the bricks to the outside face, which can mar the clean lines of the structure. It is best to waterproof the interior surface of the wall either with a plastic sheet or by applying two or three coats of waterproofing paint.

Drainage is particularly important, and weep holes, or a more elaborate system of drainage, may need to be built at the base to allow surplus water to drain away.

For brick and block beds the basic wall-building techniques described in Chapter 2 should be followed. In particular, the walled enclosure will need proper concrete foundations, and if the wall is more than about 450 mm (18 in) high it should be built one brick, or 225 mm (9 in), thick. A damp-proof course is desirable; so too is coping. Weep holes should be incorporated every 500 to 600 mm (20 to 24 in) in the base.

MASS CONCRETE walls give a smooth surface which can be colour washed to match the house. The technique involves making up smooth, well-supported shuttering, and pouring concrete into the 'mould'; curving walls, with the appropriate shuttering, are quite easy to form.

Dig a trench about 400 mm (16 in) wide and 300 mm (12 in) deep, and set up a vertical framework along the edges. The framework should be at least 75 × 50 mm (3 × 2 in) in section and spaced about every 450 to 600 mm (18 to 24 in) to prevent it bowing with the weight of concrete. The ends of the framework should preferably be driven into the trench bottom. Line the framework with marine ply 9 to 12 mm ($\frac{3}{8}$ to $\frac{1}{2}$ in) thick. The wall thickness should be about 200 mm (8 in). Join the tops of the vertical supports by nailing timbers across.

You will need to use 1:2:4 concrete (*see* Chapter 5), with a maximum aggregate size of 20 mm ($\frac{3}{4}$ in). Pour the concrete in layers of no more than 200 mm (8 in) and ram it thoroughly to achieve a dense, bubble-free wall. It is preferable that concreting is done on two occasions – the top half only when the bottom has hardened for a few days. Never pour more than about 900 mm (3 ft) in one go: the pressures involved can easily cause bowing and even failure of the shuttering. Leave the concrete to harden for at least three days before removing the shuttering.

DRY-LAID MATERIALS As already noted, you should set dry-laid materials to a batter. If you are dry-laying bricks, they will need to be of higher quality than normal, with six consistent faces, instead of common facing bricks, which have only three good sides. An attractive and effective alternative form is the dry-built brick 'tub', using 6, 8, or 10 bricks per layer depending on the size required. Using 6 bricks the tub can fit effectively on a 600 × 600 mm (2 × 2 ft) paving-slab foundation.

BLOCKS The most appropriate type is the various forms of flat, pre-cast, split-block walling that has been introduced in the last few years. Most of these need to be split immediately before use. Building to a batter is usually desirable, and a 'through-band' block penetrating some way into the soil will enhance the rigidity of the structure.

PRE-CAST SLABS Proprietary pre-cast concrete slabs, usually 900 × 300 × 50 mm (36 × 12 × 2 in), are available from various manufacturers. They are bolted together to form the raised bed. Some incorporate a pebble-dash coating; others are given a stone-block finish.

NATURAL STONE Laid dry, natural stone can make an excellent material for a raised bed. Apply the principles described in Chapter 2, in particular making sure to bond the stones well. The stones must have a wide, firm bed, and should incorporate, if possible, 'through-band' flat stones sunk well into the soil at intervals to give extra strength. Use soil as mortar, and, if desired, incorporate plants into the wall as you go, ensuring that the roots are laid into a deep area of soil.

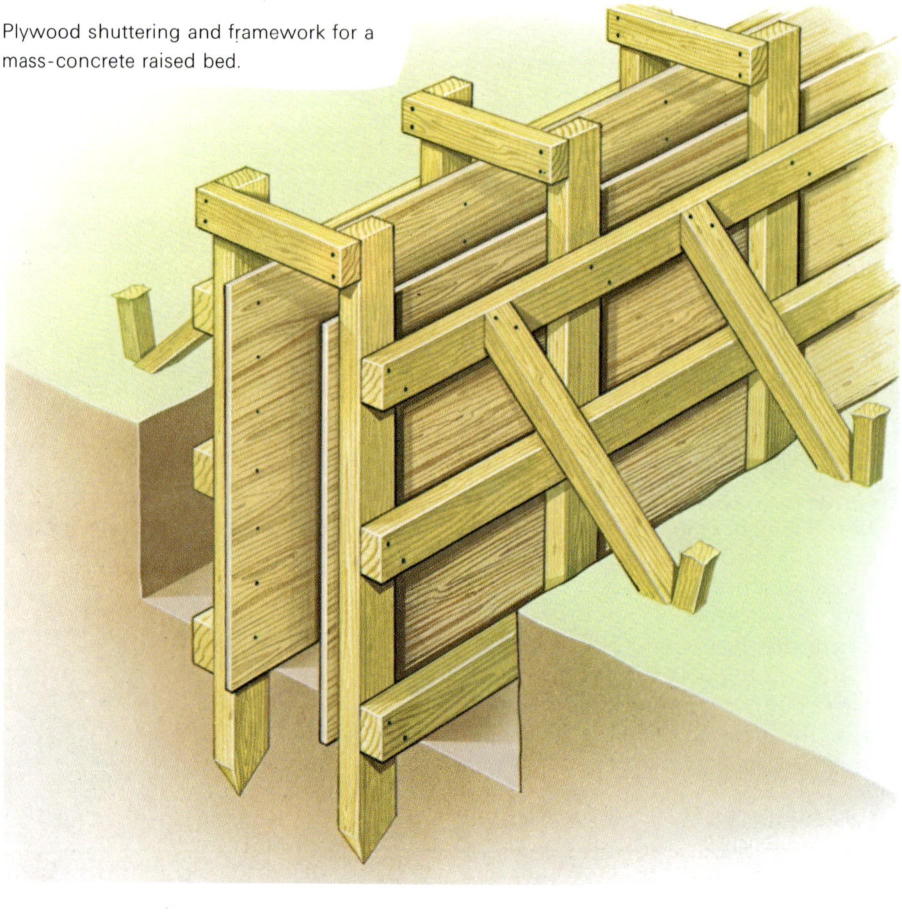

Plywood shuttering and framework for a mass-concrete raised bed.

PEAT BLOCKS These are sometimes used to form a natural, albeit temporary, raised bed. The blocks are simply bonded but should be laid to a fairly pronounced batter.

RUSTIC TIMBER Various forms are possible, but the commonest is a row of 75 mm (3 in) round or half-round stakes, driven into the ground to a depth of about 450 mm (18 in).

RAILWAY SLEEPERS These can look quite effective in the right setting. Old sleepers are generally available fairly cheaply and measure 2.8 m × 250 mm × 110 mm (8 ft 6 in × 10 in × 4½ in). They can be laid on edge or flat; the latter way, although giving a bulky effect, will provide greater stability, and also hide the unsightly holes. Indeed, the holes can be used to enhance stability if the bed is more than two sleepers high. If the holes align perfectly, you can push steel rods through consecutive sleepers and hammer them into the ground. Otherwise, if you intend to 'bond' the sleepers, drive steel spikes into the ground through the holes in the bottom layer. Then drill

Above A typical bonding system for a brick retaining wall. For extra strength the bottom six courses are 1½ bricks thick.

Below Good drainage is vital in raised beds and retaining walls, which should include weep holes (as here) at the base.

50 mm (2 in) holes into the tops of the lower course opposite the holes in the course above. Through these holes insert preserved wooden dowelling to lock the courses together.

If sleepers are placed on edge they will need to be supported. The most unobtrusive way is to set sawn-off lengths of sleeper vertically into the ground behind the main sleepers and hidden below the surface of the soil. The sleeper wall can now be fixed to the vertical supports by means of long coach screws.

Filling the bed

To minimise the effects of waterlogging it may be as well to incorporate about 150 mm (6 in) of hardcore or gravel in the bottom of the bed. On a brick wall efflorescence can be discouraged if you set a 75 mm (3 in) tile drain-line in the gravel running at a slight slope along the length of the bed and through one of the ends. This obviates the need for weep holes.

In the case of dry-laid walls, topsoil – or, better still, a topsoil/peat/sharp-sand mix – should be incorporated as the wall is built. Where concrete or mortar is used, do not fill the bed until the walls have hardened thoroughly. Mounding the soil at the top helps to show off the plants, but it may lead to staining of brickwork as a result of rainwater run-off.

Retaining walls

A retaining wall may be needed where there are to be large and steep changes of ground level. It is often wise to avoid natural steep banks, for grass slopes are difficult to mow (unless you have a hover-type mower) and the bank has a tendency to burn up in dry weather if it faces the sun. Moreover, if the bank is planted before it is properly stabilized, the topsoil (and the plants with it) may be washed away during heavy rainstorms. A retaining wall may be the only way to prevent minor local landslip if the ground on the higher part has to take considerable weights, such as parked vehicles.

The retaining wall must be designed with the greatest care, for it must be able not only to take the loading of its own mass, but also to withstand all the lateral pressures from the earth. When the soil is waterlogged these pressures can be very great, and the consequences of wall failure can be dire indeed. The best advice is always to err on the generous side as far as wall width and strength are concerned. Indeed, if the wall is much greater than 1.2 m (4 ft) high, or is built on made up or marshy ground, you would be well advised to have it designed by a structural engineer.

One way to avoid the need for a large, professionally designed retaining wall is to terrace the slope into a series of smaller retaining walls, which may not only be cheaper but aesthetically more pleasing. Another alternative is to combine a lower retaining wall with a small bank.

There are five main aspects to consider when designing a retaining wall, as follows:

STRUCTURAL STABILITY The greatest pressures will be exerted by loose, friable, sandy soils, which flow more easily than others. The wall could fail in one of two ways: it could topple forward because it is simply not strong enough; or it could be pushed forward because its base is not keyed properly into the soil. The greatest lateral pressures occur near the base. Hence, to save on materials the wall could be made triangular in cross section, and thus thicker at its base. Alternatively, the effect of the forces on the wall can be reduced by sloping the wall backwards into the soil. This has the effect of working towards the soil's natural angle of repose – the angle at which the leading edge of the bank would settle if there was no wall to support it. Whatever design you choose, the wall must have a sturdy foundation, if possible incorporating a good deep toe.

APPEARANCE Viewed from the lower level the wall will be a focal feature of the garden, and so it should be handsome as well as functional. A variety of materials can be used, including brick, blocks, natural stone, and timber. The choice should be determined by the general garden plan. It will almost certainly be worth waterproofing the back of a brick or block wall to prevent efflorescence (see page 22).

Terraced section of a stone retaining wall.

WATER DRAINAGE The greatest pressures are exerted when the soil flows easily. Waterlogging makes the soil both more fluid and heavier and greatly increases the thrust on the wall. So it is vital to provide an effective means of draining the water away. Hence drainage holes (weep holes) should be incorporated every 1 to 1.5 m (3 to 5 ft) near the base of the wall. To encourage the flow of water into the weep holes you should lay a strip of gravel about 300 mm (1 ft) wide and 300 mm deep behind the weep holes. The gravel should rest on plastic sheeting or concrete, so that the water cannot flow under the wall's foundation, lubricate the bed, and so cause the wall to slide forward. Weep holes can be made by omitting the vertical mortar joints at intervals; or you can use short lengths of 50 mm (2 in) diameter downpipe set on a slight incline.

In areas of high rainfall you would be well advised to build a properly formed concrete gulley, sloping as appropriate, at the foot of the wall to prevent water which has drained through the weep holes from spilling all over the lower ground area.

Coping made of bricks laid on their sides.

PROVIDING FOR EXPANSION Just as a long free-standing wall needs gaps to allow for expansion and contraction so, too, a long retaining wall will need a 12 mm ($\frac{1}{2}$ in) wide mastic- or fibre-filled expansion joint every 5 to 6 m (16 ft 6 in to 20 ft). To maintain the wall's strength, insert galvanized-steel rods across the joint, with one end set firmly into mortar and the other free to slide by coating it with grease.

EXTRA TOP-LOADINGS If you intend to build a driveway for cars near or along the top of the retaining wall you will need to make allowance for greatly increased lateral pressures. You would be well advised to seek professional advice on the best method to build extra strength into the wall.

Construction

The following notes apply to a typical retaining wall 1 to 1.2 m (3 to 4 ft) high. (Remember, incidentally, that if the wall is to abut a highway used by road vehicles you will probably need to obtain planning permission from your local council).

PREPARATION Dig out soil well into the slope, and angle the bank of soil to discourage it from falling on the building works during construction. Form a trench at least 400 mm (16 in) deep and 400 mm (16 in) wide, incorporating a 'toe strip' about 150 mm (6 in) deeper at the front side. Drive in pegs to establish the level for the concrete (*see* Chapter 2), then lay foundation concrete at least 150 to 200 mm (6 to 8 in) thick. Insert starter bars if the wall is to be reinforced.

BRICK A brick retaining wall should not be higher than about 1 m (3 ft) unless the bricks merely serve as cladding to a concrete structure. A solid brick wall should be 225 mm (9 in) deep, preferably incorporating piers on the front face. Added strength can be achieved by constructing the bottom six to eight courses $1\frac{1}{2}$ bricks, or 340 mm ($13\frac{1}{2}$ in) thick – the extra thickness being incorporated on the inner (soil) side of the wall. Alternatively, concrete 'deadmen' tied to the lower courses by means of reinforcing bars can be laid on the inner side.

When using bricks as a cladding to mass concrete, make the concrete wall 300 mm (12 in) wide at the base, tapering to about 200 mm (8 in) at the top. Incorporate steel rods, overlapping the starter bars, every 600 mm (2 ft) or so along the wall. If concrete is to be laid with the bricks, set a header brick into the concrete at intervals, and do not attempt to place more than a 150 to 225 mm (6 to 9 in) depth of concrete behind the bricks at any one time unless the mortar has thoroughly hardened; lateral pressures will readily dislodge the bricks, particularly when the concrete is tamped. Alternatively, of course, the mass concrete structure can be built using ordinary shuttering and the brick (or other) cladding added later. The first method, however, has the advantage of allowing you to tie the cladding into the concrete, giving extra strength.

BLOCKS The advantage of using hollow concrete blocks is that they can be reinforced. Build with 150 mm (6 in) or, better, 225 mm (9 in) hollow blocks, using one reinforcing bar, set into well-tamped concrete, every 450 mm (18 in) of wall length. Steel bars set into deadmen may also be advisable. Alternatively, you can dry-lay the blocks, set to a batter. Since such a wall would be 450 mm (18 in) thick, a large number of blocks would be needed.

STONE Always build to a batter. The choice is to use stone as facing for a reinforced-concrete structure, or to use stone by itself. The latter method will require a considerable quantity of stone because the wall will need to be at least 450 mm (18 in) wide at the base. If the wall is to be laid dry, a pronounced batter will be essential, with fairly flat, deep stones bonded well into the bank.

Completion

Proper wall coping will complete the job. The wall may finish flush with the higher level, with perhaps a flower border to decorate and emphasize change of level. Alternatively, for safety reasons (especially if you have young children), you may wish to build a small parapet – perhaps 200 to 300 mm (8 to 12 in) high – surmounted by a low fence.

5 Paths, Steps, and Patios

If used creatively, hard surfacing can increase the versatility of the garden and reduce maintenance needs. For instance, instead of a large lawn you could design a smaller lawn and a paved terrace, the advantages being that the hard-surfaced area would offer wider use throughout the year, while the smaller lawn would reduce the time you spent mowing. However, although it is good policy to be generous with areas of hard surfacing, avoid going too far and producing a desolate hard-ground cover reminiscent of a shopping precinct. In general, think about breaking up the hard-surface layout into fairly small areas, varying the surfacing materials, and incorporating plants.

The nature and design of hard surfacing should be assessed carefully in terms of functional and aesthetic qualities. In functional terms the surface may be used for access (for people, bikes, and cars), for children's play, for entertaining, and for sitting and sunbathing. The materials can vary widely according to function: a patio, for instance, should be hard, clean, smooth, quick drying, and weed-free; a path should be dry and self-draining, non slip, pleasant to walk on, and its surface should not stick to the soles of shoes. And, of course, whatever the material and the use to which it is put, it must be durable and not unreasonably expensive.

From the point of view of appearance, a potentially dull-looking hard-surfaced area can be made interesting and attractive by careful choice of colours, by breaking up the floorscape (for instance with tubs or small beds of flowers), by changing levels, and by attention to the detailed finishing both within the surfaced area and particularly at the edges. Paving materials made up of small units, such as brick pavers, can both add character and create an illusion of space within a small garden. If the same type of brick is associated with materials also used in the house or boundaries, a pleasingly co-ordinated effect may be achieved. Colour and textures are very important: bright colours that look attractive in the catalogue sometimes look garish on site, especially if they are mixed, and tend to attract the eye away from the subtle, natural colours of your plants. Large expanses of light grey concrete are not only boring to look at but can cause glare in bright sunlight. Lighter colours can help, however, to reflect light into shaded areas.

General principles

The key to success is to ensure that the hard surface is laid on a well-drained, stable base; this will avoid problems of sinkage and water-logging. All topsoil must be removed because it contains organic matter, which will decompose and may settle. The surfacing material can sometimes be laid directly onto well-compacted subsoil, but usually a well-consolidated layer of hardcore is needed, blinded with sand, ash, or hoggin (screened gravel). Plan for effective drainage of rainwater from the outset: under-drainage may be appropriate, for some materials, but always lay the surface with a fall of about 1 in 50 to prevent rainwater forming in puddles and to help the surface to dry.

Paths should be not less than 900 mm (3 ft) wide to allow access for prams, wheelbarrows, and deliveries of large objects; areas earmarked for seats should be at least 2 m (7 ft) deep.

In order to achieve a trim appearance, prevent edges falling away, and avoid soil contamination, it is usually worthwhile to make retaining edges for all hard surfaces, except possibly concrete and paving slabs. Proprietary path edgings, such as concrete edging slabs or bricks set in mortar or concrete, should be installed and their joints allowed to harden before the main surface of the path is laid.

Problems such as unevenness, sinking, or breaking up that are encountered once the surface is in regular use are nearly always due to poor foundations or bad drainage; tree roots are another potential source of trouble. Weed growths can be disfiguring as well as damaging, but can largely be prevented if you apply weedkiller before tarmac or gravel is laid.

Building a path

There is a great variety of materials available for path building, including gravel, concrete, asphalt, bricks, blocks, cobbles, and paving slabs. They offer the handyman an excellent choice in terms of cost, technical suitability, and appearance, and in larger gardens more than one type can be used.

A paved terrace and steps offer an attractive approach to this garden from the living room.

Gravel

This provides a relatively inexpensive and quickly laid surfacing material. Curves are much easier to form with gravel than with paving slabs, and slight changes in level are readily accommodated. The gravel path offers the advantage, too, that it can easily be taken up and later re-laid if underground piping and other services need to be installed beneath the path. Finally, the gravel is likely to form a good base for an alternative surface once you tire of it. The main disadvantage is that the surface is loose, and pieces of gravel spilling on to an adjacent lawn can cause serious damage to a mower.

Gravel is available in two main forms: crushed stone from quarries, and pea gravel from gravel pits. The former is of better quality, but will be very expensive unless the stone is quarried locally. According to type gravel occurs in a range of attractive colours, and your choice should if possible complement stone employed elsewhere in the garden for walling or rock gardens. The alternative, washed pea gravel, comes in shades from near white to almost black. Whichever type is used ensure that the stones are neither too large (which makes walking difficult), nor too small (they will stick to your shoes). For most purposes the best size is in the range 10 to 20 mm ($\frac{3}{8}$ to $\frac{3}{4}$ in) in diameter. Be sure that it is all of one grade; a mixture tends to settle out into layers and looks less effective.

Use of different types of material – in this case, gravel and concrete flags – lends interest to garden paths.

You need a good firm base for the best results. Once the topsoil has been removed and the land graded to take out unwanted undulations, set path edgings into concrete along the sides, apply a weedkiller that will not leach into the surrounding planted area, and put down a layer of hardcore. This can be in the form of 35 to 50 mm ($1\frac{1}{2}$ to 2 in) diameter stones or well-broken brick ends, and it must be thoroughly rammed down. For a gravel drive it is best if the layer is a little deeper, and ideally it should be consolidated with a 300 kg (6 cwt) vibrating roller. A cross fall of about 1 in 40 should be incorporated, otherwise wet areas may develop into which the gravel will sink. The hardcore should now be blinded – that is, filled and lightly covered with some finer material. If you are fortunate enough to be using local crushed stone-gravel, fine quarry waste will probably be available from the same source, and thus makes an excellent blinding. Otherwise use sharp sand or ashes. Apply sufficient blinding to fill all the spaces in the top of the hardcore, then roll it thoroughly to achieve a smooth surface on which little impression can be made with your feet. A *thin* layer of gravel, no more than 25 to 37 mm (1 to $1\frac{1}{2}$ in) thick, may now be spread and raked level. This is the secret of a good gravel path. Too many people lay the gravel thick, mistakenly assuming it will last longer. The result is that shoes and wheels sink into the layer, making ruts and throwing up stones. Correctly laid, a gravel path will need only an occasional raking, and maybe sweeping to tidy it up at the edges.

Concrete

Used in mass form as a garden surfacing material, concrete is hard, durable, and fairly easy to lay, and once laid it is more or less permanent. To many people, the colour of concrete is harsh, to others merely boring; certainly large, bare areas of concrete are pretty unexciting. Colouring agents can help to relieve the monotony if the concreted area is fairly small and the colours chosen with care, but a much more interesting effect can be achieved by modifying the surface texture – for example, by exposing the coarse stone aggregate.

Contrary to popular belief, concrete can be laid directly on to a suitable subsoil. Thus, once the topsoil has been removed, and if the subsoil is firm and stable, the only preparation necessary is to grade the ground to the appropriate falls for drainage, and then to roll it thoroughly. Any soft spots should be dug out and replaced with rammed hardcore.

If the subsoil is not so suitable a 75 to 150 mm (3 to 6 in) layer of well-rolled hardcore will be needed – the thickest layer being required in the case of a driveway for cars. Blind the hardcore with sharp sand – or hoggin, which is cheaper – and roll thoroughly. To aid drainage incorporate a 1:40 cross fall over the path or drive.

You will now need to set shuttering, or formwork, at the sides to retain the concrete when it is poured and keep it straight at the edges. Special steel shuttering and holding pins can be hired, but a cheaper alternative is to use old planks of timber, at least 25 mm (1 in) thick, set along the edges and held in place with pegs. The finished thickness of the concrete for a path will need to be about 75 mm (3 in) and for a drive up to 150 mm (6 in), and the shuttering planks must be wide enough to accommodate these thicknesses. The cross fall can be achieved by resting a lath, the thickness of which is equal to the fall, on one of the formwork sides. Set a straight edge and spirit level across between the formwork, and bang the shuttering down on the lath side with a mallet until a level reading is achieved on the spirit level.

Concrete is a mixture of cement, (usually ordinary Portland cement), sharp (concreting) sand, stones, and water. For good-quality concrete the proportions of these materials should be carefully measured and mixed. Always store the materials separately, and use heavy-duty plastic buckets to measure the ingredients (measuring by shovelfuls is not accurate enough). Never lay concrete in frosty weather.

Stone, usually called 'coarse aggregate', comes in various sizes, depending on the thickness of concrete to be laid and the smoothness of finish desired. Commonly the stone is 20 mm ($\frac{3}{4}$ in) in diameter, but for thin concrete sections and for very fine surfaces use 10 mm ($\frac{3}{8}$ in) stone.

The standard mix (Mix A, below) is 1 part of cement, $2\frac{1}{2}$ parts of sharp sand, and 4 parts of 20 mm ($\frac{3}{4}$ in) stone. For thinner sections a richer mix (Mix B) of 1 : 2 : 3, using 10 to 12 mm ($\frac{3}{8}$ to $\frac{1}{2}$ in) stone, is recommended. The quantities needed for 1 m³ (1.3 cu yd) of concrete are:

	Mix A	*Mix B*
Portland cement (50 kg bags)	6 bags	7 bags
Damp sharp sand	0.5 m³	0.5 m³
Stone	0.8 m³	0.75 m³

There are two ways of mixing – by hand, and using a mechanical concrete mixer; or you can have the concrete delivered ready mixed. Manual mixing is recommended only for concreting small areas – it is exhausting work. You will need a smooth, firm surface (such as the garage floor) and a good strong shovel. Measure out the materials into a pile, preferably adding the cement last of all, and move the pile at least three times, turning it all over, until it is a uniform grey colour. Form a dip in the middle of the pile and add some of the water. As a guide, you will need about one half to two thirds of a bucket of water for every bucket of cement. Shovel dry mix into the 'pond' in the middle until it dries up, and thoroughly turn the pile over. Be sparing with the water because a wet, sloppy mix will be weak and give a poor surface. Add water until the mix is all wetted but remains fairly stiff. If you have accidentally added too much water, a little more dry mix must be added.

For all but minor jobs, you will be well advised to hire a concrete mixer, normally driven by a petrol engine or electric motor (*see* Chapter 9). After starting the mixer pour in half the

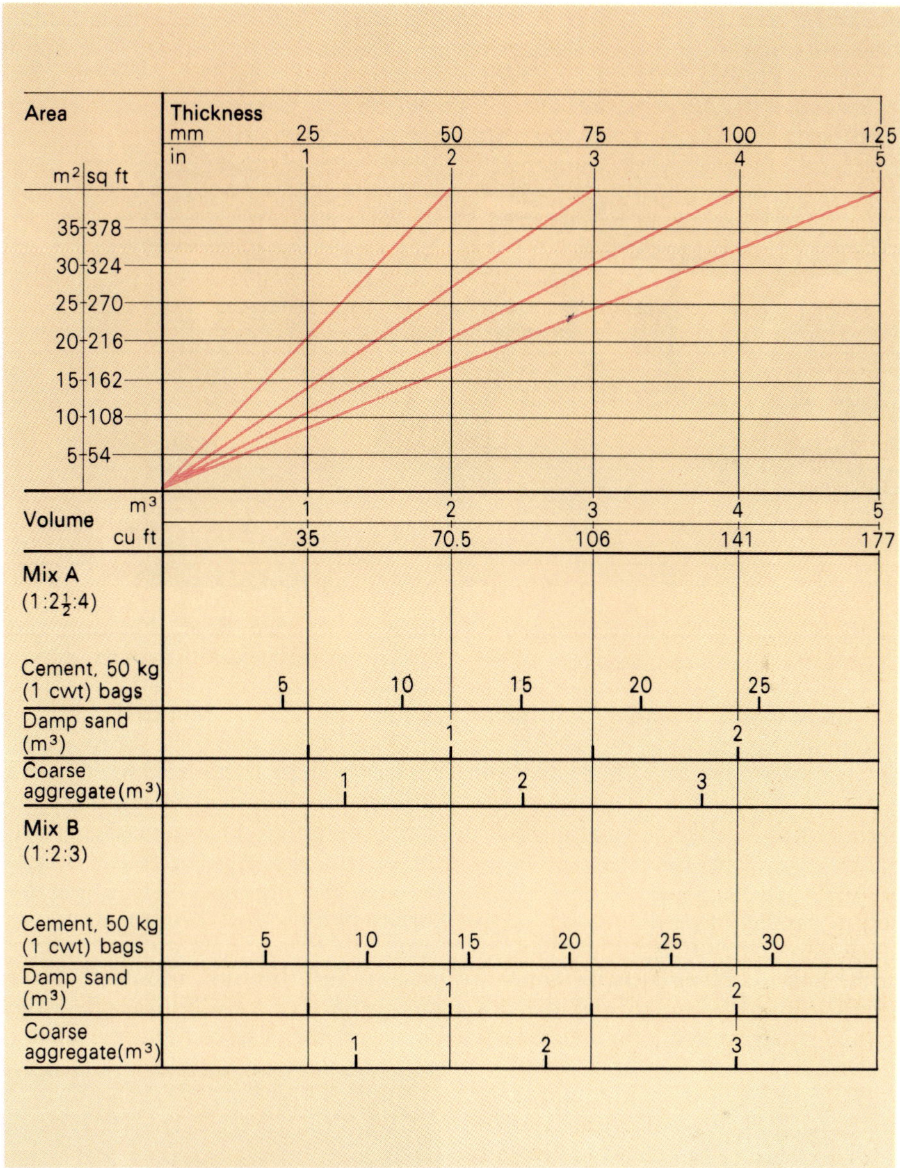

aggregate and water, then add all the sand. Let them mix for about two minutes before adding the cement, followed by the remaining aggregate and enough water to give the desired consistency. Mix the concrete for a further three minutes, then tip it into a wheelbarrow.

You buy convenience with ready mixed concrete, and although it is commonly more expensive you do not have to clutter up the garden with piles of sand and gravel. The key points to bear in mind are that you must be well organized and must provide a good access for the mixer lorry near the area you intend to concrete. Work out the exact quantities of sand, gravel, and cement you need, and stipulate the precise time it must be delivered. Have plenty of helpers available: the lorry will be delivering all the concrete at once, and it needs to be laid within two hours, so you will need at least two wheelbarrows to bring the concrete to the path or driveway area.

Even if you are mixing your own concrete you would be well advised to enlist the help of at least one other person. It is heavy work, and it is a common mistake to over-estimate the amount of concrete that can be laid in one session.

Concrete expands in the heat of summer and contracts in winter, so joints must be incorporated at intervals to allow it to expand without cracking. Concrete can be laid either in a continuous strip or in parallel bays; but whichever method is used,

Laying a concrete driveway. The builders have omitted to use expansion joints.

the joints should be inserted at intervals not greater than 2.5 m (8 ft). With the continuous method, thin softwood laths can be used as joints and left permanently in place, or you can obtain proprietary fibreboard strips from builders' merchants. If the concrete is laid in parallel bays, the same type of expansion/contraction strip can be used, or the softwood board can be removed afterwards and the gap filled with black mastic. An expansion joint is necessary, too, where the concrete abuts a wall.

When you have poured the concrete, roughly level it with a shovel until it is about 15 to 20 mm ($\frac{3}{8}$ to $\frac{3}{4}$ in) proud of the formwork. With the assistance of a helper tamp (compress) the concrete using a piece of timber – a length of 100 × 50 mm (4 × 2 in) section will do. Progress slowly along the newly laid concrete, using a tapping action to compress it. Every metre or so, back track and use the tamper in a sawing action to remove high spots. Remove surplus concrete with a shovel, fill any low spots, and tamp again. Avoid over-tamping, because this will bring too much water to the top, producing a weak, powdery surface when the concrete hardens.

Once compressed, the concrete must be given an appropriate surface finish. A steel float can be employed to give the smoothest finish – but this can be dangerously slippery for a path. A slightly rougher effect can be achieved using a wooden float. Floating the surface should be done delicately, drawing the float lightly in a series of semicircular sweeps. A textured effect is produced by drawing a broom across the surface half an hour or so after the concrete has been laid. A light broom will give a less pronounced texture than a stiff one. Aggregate can be exposed to pleasing effect by brushing the surface with a soft broom about an hour after laying, then somewhat later with a stiff broom, followed by a hosing off. For a really neat effect the edges of the slab should be finally smoothed, using a 75 mm (3 in) wide home-made float, angling it slightly towards the edge.

Concrete should not be allowed to dry out too quickly; the longer moisture is retained, the stronger the concrete will be. In hot, windy conditions the drying rate may be so fast as to encourage hairline cracks to form in the concrete surface. To help the concrete dry at the optimum rate, cover the surface with a polythene sheet held down at the edges, and leave it in place for three to five days. Do not walk on the concrete during this period, and allow driveways for vehicles to dry for several more days before use.

Coated macadam (asphalt)

This material consists of stone coated with a binder of tar or bitumen, and is widely used in road making. Its advantages for paths and drives are that it can be laid speedily in a thinner layer than concrete, and that it is somewhat easier to repair. The two most important things to ensure are that the stone is mixed with the correct amount of binder and that it is adequately compacted when it is laid. Failure in either case can lead to the macadam breaking up in winter or softening in summer.

Coated macadam is available in a

Coated macadam driveway. Hard edges help to reduce maintenance and look neat.

number of grades which provide open, medium, or fine textures. Open-texture types are used only for the base course, while medium- and fine-textured forms are used as the top or wearing surface. Fine-textured coated macadam contains fine aggregate of a nominal size of 6 mm ($\frac{1}{4}$ in) or less; while medium-textured types contain about 25 per cent fine aggregate, the remainder being of larger sizes. Tar and bitumen are usually mixed together as the binder; if oil drips from the car are likely to be a problem it is better to use a binder with a higher tar content.

Most coated macadams are laid hot because the binder is soft when hot and stiff when dry; when it is laid in cold weather or if the job is to be extended over a couple of days, a fluxing oil is often added to keep the binder workable as it cools.

You can tackle the job in one of three ways: by using coated macadam bought from a local coating plant; by using pre-packed bags of coated macadam; and by contracting the work out to a professional. If you choose the third way (and many enthusiastic handymen are reluctant to lay macadam) make sure that you get a quotation in writing with a complete specification, preferably stipulating the use of British Standard materials. Whether you are doing the job yourself or contracting the work, adequate preparatory work is essential (and must be specified if you are getting a quotation). This includes excavation of the site, application of weedkiller, laying consolidated hardcore, and kerbing. For a drive, the best result is achieved if the macadam is applied in two layers: a base course of open texture about 50 mm (2 in) thick, and a wearing-surface layer of fine texture 15 to 20 mm ($\frac{5}{8}$ to $\frac{3}{4}$ in) thick. Both courses must be thoroughly rolled.

When tackling the job yourself, prepare the site as described for a gravel path or drive. For blinding the hardcore, well rolled hoggin can be used. Order the macadam from the coating plant: for a wearing surface of about 20 mm ($\frac{3}{4}$ in) thick 1,000 kg (1 ton) will cover 20 to 24 m² (24 to 29 sq yd). For a large area try to arrange delivery of the macadam in batches, so that a fresh load arrives just as you are completing laying the previous one. You will need hot rakes and forks, a brazier to heat them up, a tarpaulin to keep the macadam heap warm, a straight edge, a vibrating roller, a watering can – and plenty of help.

Carefully spread out the macadam with forks and rake it level. Use the straight edge to remove high and low spots. When you are satisfied that the surface is level, roll it two or three times with the vibrating roller, sprinkling water over the roller if the macadam tends to stick to it. This is important, for low spots cannot effectively be filled after you have rolled the surface. Remember that you have limited working time, and that once the macadam cools it is very difficult to work.

Pre-packed, black, green, or red coated macadams are available from builders' merchants. They are laid cold, and, because the fluxing oils used to make the macadam workable evaporate slowly, they take a much longer time to harden than the hot-laid material. Many of these proprietary macadams begin to harden in the bag after six months, so make sure that you buy fresh material. The method of preparation and laying is similar to that used for hot macadam, except that hot tools are not needed; however, the job is more easily done in warm weather. So long as you take care that the laid macadam is thoroughly levelled with a straight edge, you can probably produce an adequately compacted surface with a normal but heavy (preferably water-filled) garden roller.

Bricks and blocks

Bricks are not widely used as paving because of the cost involved and the time needed to lay them. However, if they are carefully laid, bricks of the appropriate texture and pattern can give a very pleasing appearance indeed, especially on fairly short paths. The fact that the path will lie wet for long periods means that not all bricks

Brick and stone paths offer scope for a variety of patterns and colours.

are suitable. Hard, dense, impermeable types should be used; they must be frost resistant and not prone to efflorescence (*see* Chapter 2). Engineering bricks are mostly suitable, but stick to mellow colours. The bricks can be laid either on their side or flat: the latter way is cheaper, but make sure that the top surfaces have a suitable finish: on many facing bricks only the sides and ends are suitable for exposure. A variety of paver bricks is available, and some of them incorporate patterns in their surface. In the last few years special concrete paver blocks, in various shapes and colours, have come on the market.

One of the attractions of using such bricks or blocks is that they can be laid in a wide variety of patterns to create visual interest, and sometimes also an illusion of extra space, width, or depth. Since there is some variation in the size of bricks it is best not to attempt a too elaborate pattern, otherwise the bricks may require trimming. Herringbone patterns will entail the cutting of bricks or blocks diagonally at the edges.

The first task is to prepare a 75 to 100 mm (3 to 4 in) thick consolidated hardcore base blinded with sand. Make sure that the base is completely flat and incorporates a 1 in 50 or 1 in 60 fall. Manufacturers recommend that block pavers are laid on to sand; bricks can also be laid on sand, but they are more usually laid on a mix containing one part of cement to every four of sand.

Always install edging before you lay the bricks or blocks. The edging can be either of timber (which can be left in position) or, better, a row of bricks set on end in mortar; alternatively, lay a row of bricks on their sides at a slightly lower level than the main path.

Set the paving bricks into a well levelled 37 to 50 mm ($1\frac{1}{2}$ to 2 in) layer of mortar and tap them down gently, checking with a straight edge that all are being set to the same level. Leave a 10 mm ($\frac{3}{8}$ in) gap between each brick for grouting and to allow for tolerances in brick sizes.

Grouting bricks is a little tricky. You must at all costs avoid staining the bricks with mortar, so use a dryish mix tamped down with a stick. Finish the joints with a piece of bent rod so that the mortar is just below the brick

The severity of concrete slabs contrasts effectively with informal plantings.

surface. Clean each brick with a damp, well-rinsed cloth before proceeding.

An alternative method is to grout with a dry mix, and then to water the bricks from a watering can or slow-running hose, scrubbing each brick in the process and smoothing each joint with the rod. Cure the joints periodically with a light spray of water for the next two or three days. Concrete-block pavers are easier to lay and grout. Once all the blocks have been laid in position they should be consolidated, preferably by using a hired plate vibrator. Finally, sand is swept into the joints, and the surplus cleaned from the surface.

Cobbles

These smooth, rounded stones, from about 25 mm (1 in) diameter upwards, are attractive when used on a small scale, or as an interesting infilling material (around a tree, for instance) where it might be difficult to cut larger paving materials. With patience and thought, all kinds of interesting patterns can be created using various shapes of cobbles.

The technique of laying is quite simple. They should be packed together as close as possible in a bed of mortar or concrete on a hardcore base. Ensure that the cobble surface is not contaminated with mortar. Alternatively set them into a dry bed of mortar or concrete and water them in with a sprinkler.

Paving materials: coloured concrete, small granite blocks, and natural stone.

Proprietary-paving slabs made of reconstituted stone are available in many sizes, shapes, and colours.

Paving slabs

These are the most commonly used materials for hard surfacing in the garden. Prefabricated concrete slabs are available in a vast range of colours and textures, and vary in shape from the 600 × 600 mm (2 × 2 ft) common grey slab to polygonal and circular forms. Most are 50 mm (2 in) thick or less. The more expensive types are made of reconstituted stone, and some are available in a texture reminiscent of water-worn stone. It is important that the surface finish is non-slip: a smooth finish encrusted with algal growth can be treacherous in wet weather.

It is quite easy to make your own paving slabs, and if you construct a wooden framework from 50 × 50 mm (2 × 2 in) section timber with multiple 'cells' you can form several slabs at once. Use a 1:2:3 mix of cement, sharp sand, and stone of a nominal size no larger than 10 mm ($\frac{3}{8}$ in). Place the framework on to a polythene sheet laid on a clean smooth surface and pour in the concrete. An alternative to polythene is hessian-based building paper, which will give a slight texturing effect. Tamp the concrete well to achieve a bubble-free slab surface.

There are a number of ways in which slabs can be laid but, whichever method is chosen, a firm, well-prepared base is needed. When the subsoil has been graded to the correct fall, put down a 75 mm (3 in) layer of consolidated hardcore or ash, ram it down, and blind it with sand, ash, or quarry waste. Get the levels exactly right. If the slabs are to abut a lawn, either set them about 10 to 12 mm ($\frac{3}{8}$ to $\frac{1}{2}$ in) lower than the lawn for simple machine mowing; or, if you have an edge-trimming machine, set the slabs 50 to 60 mm (2 to $2\frac{1}{2}$ in) below lawn level.

If there is no danger of washing out by rainwater, the slabs can be laid on a 25 to 50 mm (1 to 2 in) layer of sand only; but a more permanent method, less liable to settlement, is to bed in mortar or concrete.

Whatever material is used for bedding, be careful to level it out with a screeding board, and then gently compress it. Alternatively, place dots of bedding material immediately under the corners and the centre of each slab. Now carefully lower each slab into place. If you are using the larger 900 × 600 mm (3 × 2 ft) slabs, this is definitely work for two people, not one. Tap each slab down lightly, using a piece of wood to cushion the blow and prevent cracking, until there is no tendency for the slab to rock. Now use a straight edge to check that the general paving level is correct before proceeding. Be prepared to take up slabs and adjust the levels if you are not satisfied.

Leave a joint of about 12 mm ($\frac{1}{2}$ in) between the slabs, and grout with a wet or dry 1:4 cement/soft sand mix in the way described for brick pavers. Remove any mortar that gets on to the slabs before it dries.

Try to plan the paving in such a way that you will not have to cut any of the slabs; cutting is tricky work. One way is to lay the slab to be cut on a bed of sand and to tap along the cutting line with a hammer and bolster chisel, preferably on both sides of the slab. Continue tapping around the slab, making the blows progressively heavier until the slab cracks along the desired line.

For curving paths the radius infills can be formed of screeded mortar, perhaps with small pebbles set into the surface, or left to grass. You could make your own radius slabs if you wish, but you may find it impossible to match the colour and texture of the other slabs.

Right A hired plate vibrator is invaluable for consolidating brick or other pavers.

Steps

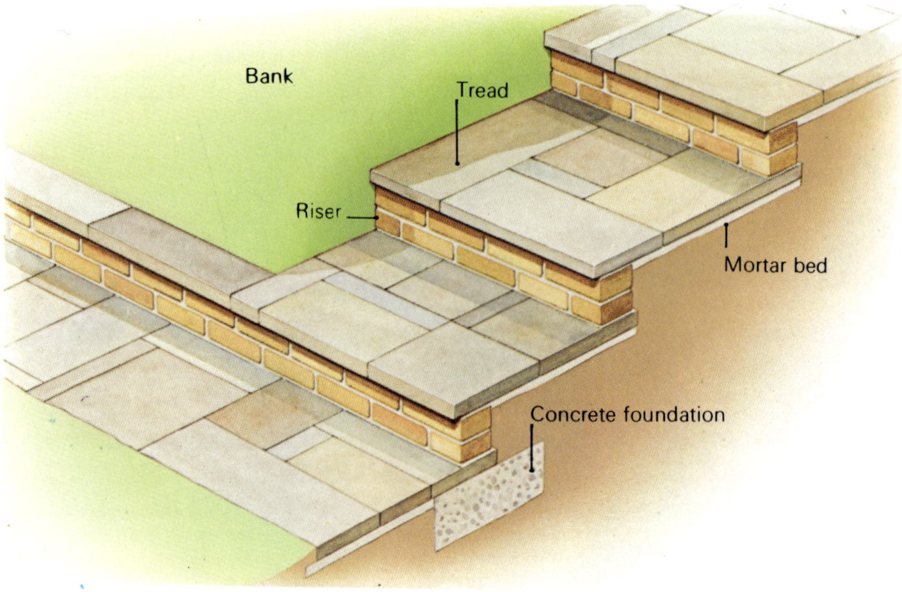

Garden steps should be more than functional: with careful design they can be made an attractive focal point. Obviously, the materials used should match or complement adjacent hard surfacing. It is customary for slabs to be used for the treads, with brick, block, or stone risers; but all-brick or concrete steps can be formed. In certain circumstances, informal log steps make a suitable alternative. Quite as important as the choice of materials is the scale, both of the structure as a whole and of the individual steps. Progress up and down should be leisurely and easy. Even if only a few steps are required, allow for plenty of width – wide steps can look very attractive.

The 'going' (the distance from the front to the back of each step) should be about 450 mm (18 in) and certainly not less than 300 mm (12 in). The risers should be 100 to 150 mm (4 to 6 in) and never more than 200 mm (8 in). In other words the total flight should be between two and three times as long as it is high. The number of steps required can be calculated after measurement of the height and angle of the slope. To avoid having to cut your building materials, try to work to exact courses of bricks or blocks and slab heights. The steps, incidentally, need not follow a steep slope precisely; they can, for instance, be built out at the bottom or cut into the bank at the top. It is always desirable to produce a scale section diagram before you begin work. More ambitious schemes can include a curving flight of steps. Pleasant finishing touches, such as hollow piers for plants on either side of the steps, add neatly to the overall effect.

Construction

The steps have three main components: treads, risers, and retaining side walls (the last, although attractive, are not always necessary; for details of construction, *see* Chapter 4).

Begin with the bottom step by setting a tread into the ground at the lowest level. It is possible to omit this first tread, but it improves the scale of the structure and, if the steps serve a lawn, this slab will help to protect the grass. Lay courses of bricks, blocks, or

stone for the first riser near the back edge of the first tread, and ensure that the top line of the riser is perfectly level. Clear out some of the soil behind the riser, and if it is soft introduce a compacted layer of hardcore blinded with sand. Spread a layer of 1:4 mortar and bed the next tread with a 10 to 12 mm ($\frac{3}{8}$ to $\frac{1}{2}$ in) fall to the front. The front of the slab should project 25 mm (1 in) forward of its riser. Build the remaining steps in a similar manner.

Ramps

A ramp is useful if lawnmowers, wheelbarrows, and suchlike are frequently moved from one level to the next. The slope should be a gradual one, preferably no more than 1 in 10. Most materials are suitable except gravel, which is too loose: it is vital that a good grip is incorporated into the ramp surface.

Left, above, and right Contrasting forms and slopes of garden steps.

Patios

Patios are usually paved with pre-cast paving slabs, although to reduce the materials cost it may be possible to buy broken slabs from the local council for making up into crazy paving.

Consider closely what type of pre-cast slab will suit your purpose, for there is a bewildering choice of shapes, colours, and textures. Colours should be chosen with great care, and it is almost invariably best to choose fairly subdued, natural-looking tones. A single colour usually looks best in a small patio; more than two colours tend to look garish even in a large one. Choose slabs that are coloured all the way through: surface-coloured slabs are usually a false economy because the colour is eventually worn away. Check that the colour of your choice is as attractive to you when the slab is wet as when it is dry.

Design

Begin by drawing a scale plan on which is marked the lines of all the drains and positions of manholes and water pipes; mark the areas within or immediately bordering the patio where you wish to make plantings. Now, using manufacturers' plans and leaflets work out an appropriate layout using standard sizes (to avoid having to cut slabs); if the site is to be terraced, make provision for steps, ramps, and retaining walls.

Manhole covers present a problem because it is against building regulations to cover them right up. If you are fortunate enough to be planning the patio before the drains are laid, ask that the manholes are sited to suit you. Otherwise, a manhole can be disguised by placing a plant container or training a prostrate plant over it, to be pushed back when access is needed. Sometimes it is possible to use a special recessed manhole cover, into the top of which appropriately cut paving is fixed. It is generally possible for the height of the manhole cover to be adjusted to suit the desired patio level by adding or removing a layer of bricks within the inspection chamber. If none of these alternatives is possible you may have to re-lay drains in a more convenient position. Your local building inspector will need to be informed about this.

A simple plan and realization of a patio for a small garden.

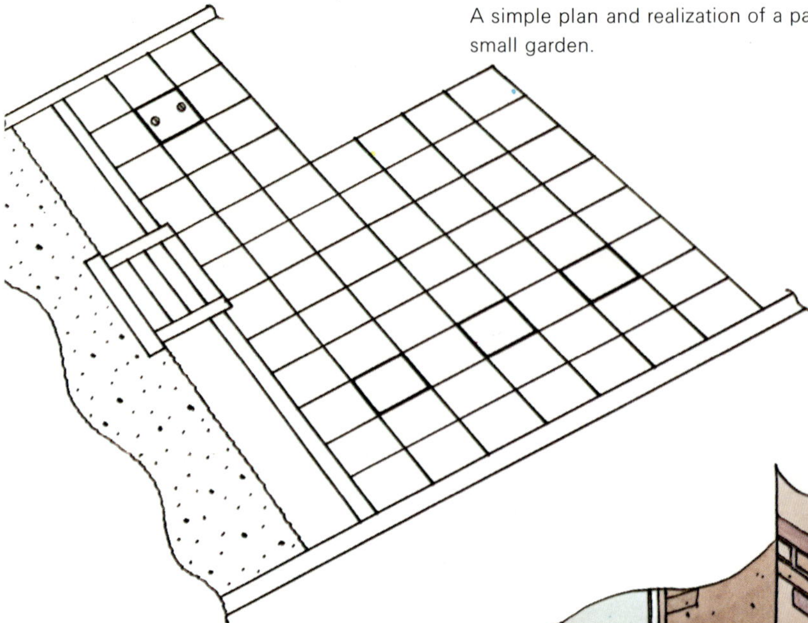

Different approaches to the design of a patio. **Below** In the typical small town garden, space is at a premium and the paved area, which is likely to be intensively used, needs to be well defined and uncluttered. **Left** Large country gardens invite a more expansive approach; the paving may cover a greater area and the margins of the patio can be allowed to merge informally with the surroundings.

Laying and Slabs

The finished level of the patio must be not less than 150 mm (6 in) below the house damp-proof course, so it may be necessary to remove old concrete or other laid surfacing. Never cover up house air vents.

Clear the top soil and level the site generally. Drive in a series of level pegs around the site (as described in Chapter 2 for the preparation of wall foundations) using a datum peg, straight edge, and spirit level. All the pegs should be driven in until their tops are at the same level; the more pegs you use, the more uniform you will be able to make the surface. A fall of about 1 in 100 or so from the house must be incorporated; for a patio 3 m (10 ft) deep this means that the outermost slabs will be about 30 mm ($1\frac{1}{4}$ in) lower than those abutting the house wall, so you must adjust

Left Clearing the site. **Below left** Laying a slab. The wooden spacers form uniform joints for pointing. **Below** Level laying is achieved here by stretching a line between the two end slabs, which were laid first.

the peg tops to accommodate this.

Lay hardcore about 75 to 100 mm (3 to 4 in) deep and firm it well, preferably with a vibrating roller. Blind the surface with sand raked level, and roll again. Slabs can now be laid on to a mortar bed, as previously described. Keep the joints in line and check continuously with a straight edge that the slabs are laid uniformly in all planes and that they are flush with one another. An uneven surface is not only dangerous but unsightly, and it will tend to collect puddles. Remove the level pegs as you go along. Complete the job by pointing the joints with neatly smoothed mortar infill, and keep off the slabs for about five days.

If the patio is a large size you may need to make a small gutter along the lower side to lead rainwater to a drain and soakaway.

An air of intimacy in town gardens can be achieved by enclosing the patio with tall-growing plants. Flowering plants in tubs or troughs can be used to provide points of vivid colour.

6 Rock Gardens

A rock garden is essentially an informal setting of rocks encompassing a collection of alpine and other plants. It should as far as possible resemble a natural rock outcrop, with little soil showing and a fairly thick covering of plant life thriving in conditions reminiscent of their natural habitat. The rocks should therefore be arranged to simulate a natural formation: any semblance of man-made uniformity should be avoided. The growing medium should be suitable to support alpines, which are mostly natives of high mountain crags of the Alps and Himalayas.

The essential need of a rock garden is to provide just sufficient moisture for the needs of alpines in the summer, and very good drainage and protection from lying damp in the winter. Many alpines have long roots which penetrate deep into rock crevices and into moist pockets of soil under and behind rocks. Moisture loss from the thin soil in the rock garden can be reduced to some extent by a covering of fine gravel.

Before planning your layout pay a visit to a well-thought-out rock garden, study it carefully, and then consider what is entailed. Whilst a fall is not essential, a rock garden can often make the best use of a slope; a flat site, on the other hand, can be effectively developed to simulate, say, an undulating alpine meadow. The size of your rock garden will depend primarily on the amount of space you have available and, secondarily, on the sizes of the stones to be used. But alpine plants are mostly quite small, so that even corners can be transformed into a worthwhile, interesting miniature rock garden.

The cost will largely depend on the local availability of suitable stone, access by lorries, and handling costs generally. Remember that, once established, the rock garden is a more or less permanent feature – so it pays to get it right first time.

A suitable backdrop enhances the overall appearance of the rock garden – and brick walls or other man-made structures, are inappropriate. Natural surroundings in the form of a hedge or shrubs are preferable, and a sloping site, as long as it is not too steep, is particularly effective (very steep slopes suffer from soil erosion in wet weather). Most rock plants require an open, sunny site, but they should not be exposed to full sunlight all day. Do not establish the garden too near trees, for not only do they create shade but drips from leaves can harm the damp, sensitive alpines. For those plants requiring shelter, shade can be provided in the lee of the rocks.

It is essential that the soil and site are well drained, and water must be allowed to move through the soil and then to escape. Wet areas can be turned to good effect by creating pools, streams, and waterfalls.

Site preparation

Dig out all perennial weeds, particularly those that are deep rooted and those that spread readily. The site must now be fashioned ready to receive the rocks. Mark out the area with pegs, and if space allows incorporate a path so that there is access to all parts of it. Decide on the shape you want and begin the excavation. Dig no deeper than 500 to 700 mm (20 to 28 in); avoid narrow, steep dips, which will not only appear contrived but will be prone to erosion.

Leave hollows where the rocks are to be set, and if the soil is somewhat soft install a well-compacted layer of hardcore for the heavier rocks.

Use local stone if possible; try to get weather-worn stone rather than newly quarried material. You will find it more convenient to work with a sample containing wide, flat, more or less rectangular shapes than those that are cubical or pyramidal. Sandstones and limestones are the best, and they weather well.

It is essential to use a fairly porous stone, with cracks and crevices in which roots of plants can seek coolness and moisture. Such stone, sometimes, is also capable of hand fashioning so that holes may be gouged out into which soil is packed to support an appropriate plant. Hard, impermeable rocks such as granite are inappropriate in the rock garden.

A special form of very porous limestone called tufa is available; this is particularly suitable for the miniature rock garden. An explanatory leaflet on tufa is available from the Royal Botanic Gardens, Kew. The material is white to creamy yellow in colour, and because of its porous nature drainage is excellent, although it can hold enough moisture for plant growth. It is com-

A mature rock garden on a natural slope.

paratively easy to form holes for planting in blocks of this material. A man-made 'rock' material called Literoc is available with a sandstone-type finish. The 'rocks' are hollow and consequently are comparatively easy to handle. Some garden pools and cascades are manufactured from this material.

Setting the stones

Hauling and setting stones is heavy work, so take no risks. Suitable rocks can be well over 100 kg (2 cwt), and large specimens are best moved by rolling them or using crowbars, rollers, or a plank track consisting of a flat board and rollers. Be particularly careful on sloping sites. Smaller rocks can be moved using a wheelbarrow, preferably with pneumatic tyres.

The use of mortar should not be necessary in setting the rocks, but where, in the occasional spot, it is considered desirable, it should not be exposed to view.

The two essentials when laying the rocks is to place them in a natural-looking relation to each other and to create realistic strata (layers). Remember that in nature each rock is part of a given rock mass and the strata of which the rocks are formed should all lie in the same direction.

The formation should look attractive in all seasons and from all sides, so a great deal of care needs to go into the selection and setting of the rocks. Avoid spacing the rocks in a uniform pattern.

Begin by sorting out the larger and more attractive rocks, and select the finest one as the keystone. Set it up on its nose, and examine it from all angles, for its position and appearance will influence those of all the other rocks.

The rocks should be set well into the ground, often to at least half their depth, and they should be tilted backwards slightly, which will allow rainwater to trickle back into the slope under the rock to feed the roots of plants. If the rocks tilt forward, plant roots will be sheltered from rain, and in the highly porous growing medium plants can easily die off in such conditions.

The appearance is enhanced if the best face of the stone is fairly well exposed, and with the opposite face embedded into well-packed soil. By using a gently sloping terrace in front of these rocks for planting, you will help to minimise soil erosion during heavy rainstorms.

Constructing a rock garden. **Above** The larger stones can be manoeuvred into position with wood or steel crowbars and plank tracks. **Right** Pack the soil against and between the stones, leaving the best face of each exposed.

Neither pile up rocks steeply on top of one another, nor space them out so far that they look like currants in a bun. If you run short of larger stones, group three or four smaller stones together; such a combination can be made to resemble the partially exposed outcrop of one large boulder.

Preparation for planting

Unimpeded drainage is vital for success, so any consolidation of the soil resulting from movement of larger stones must be made good by forking. Where the soil lacks porosity, a drainage layer of small rubble, gravel, and sand is recommended. For heavy clay soil this should be 300 to 400 mm (12 to 16 in) deep. Only a thin layer of soil is needed on top, but it should have a good organic-matter content. On lighter, more porous soil all that may be necessary is for fine gravel and the organic, humus-forming materials to be mixed into the top layer.

To simulate the scree effect of a moraine it is usual for soil to be covered with chippings – small enough to be pushed aside by a shoot, but in sufficient numbers to prevent drying of the earth. This will also improve drainage of the surface and help to keep it stable.

Special attention should be paid to filling crevices and cracks between rocks. Pack in drainage material, followed by a growing medium into which plantings can be made.

Rock beds

Most of the basic principles previously described apply also to these miniature rock gardens, except that smaller stones will need to be used, and space will probably rule out the formation of an outcrop. Use stones no larger than an individual can lift comfortably – about 25 kg (55 lb). Form a low mound and place larger stones at the base adjacent to the path, burying them to half their depth. Set the surface fairly thickly with stones of varying sizes and avoid forming any definite pattern. Group stones here and there, and set some rocks further into the soil than others.

Paths

For rock gardens, paths should be informal and their edges should merge imperceptibly with the surroundings. Small rocks make excellent edging material, while the paths can be surfaced with matching flat rocks, gravel, or broken paving.

Left When the stones are in position and a good drainage layer applied, add a growing mixture to the topsoil. **Above** Planting out. Exploit the crevices between the rocks as well as the soil immediately in front of the exposed faces.

7 Water Features

Ornamental water features – pools, waterfalls and fountains – add considerable life and interest to many gardens. Still water can be used to mirror the vertical landscape around it or can be covered with exotic plant life; moving water can sparkle, catching the sun and producing delightful murmuring and splashing sounds. Waterfalls are perhaps seen at their best when set within a rock garden.

Water features are not, however, suitable for every garden. Space is a primary requirement, for a tiny area of still water looks mean, and there may be insufficient expanse to obtain reflections. Pools are best sited away from trees, which can cause serious pollution with rotting leaves in the autumn. Safety is also an important consideration: young children are fascinated by water, and would need to be constantly supervised when playing by a garden pool.

It is a good idea to visit a water-garden centre to get inspiration for your own design and to see for yourself what is involved. Two of the finest centres are at Nantwich in Cheshire and at Enfield in Middlesex.

Pools

A formal pool is geometric in shape – square, rectangular, or circular – and is usually the centrepiece of a formal paved area such as a patio. Many garden pools, however, are informal in style – irregular in shape and intended to form part of the natural landscape. Which style you choose is up to you – but the pool obviously should be compatible with the character of the garden.

Correct siting is perhaps the most vital factor influencing the general impact which a pool will have upon the garden scene. Often the site will be dictated by the existing layout, but it should always receive at least half a

day's sunlight, preferably more, and it must be away from trees. A level site is not necessary, for it is fairly straightforward to install a pool on gently sloping ground and to retain soil above and below it with rocks. The pool itself, however, must be perfectly level, for it is unsightly to have water up to the rim at one end and a large expanse of lining showing at the other.

Space and cost normally limit the size, but try to keep it in proportion to the surrounding area. It is commonly recommended that in order to obtain natural harmony between water, plants, and fish, a minimum surface area of 3.5 m^2 (38 sq ft) is required. If the pool is much smaller than this the water may remain cloudy and dirty looking. The recommended depth is between 375 and 600 mm (15 and 24 in), with a planting shelf some 230 mm (9 in) below the surface and 230 mm (9 in) wide around the margin of the pool. Water less than 375 mm (15 in) deep is prone to overheating in hot weather, and may leave the fish short of oxygen; it may also freeze solid in winter.

The shape chosen is a matter of preference: but do not get carried away and design too elaborate or irregular a shape, which may be difficult to build. Stick to bold curves; the most convenient is a variant of the basic kidney shape. To get a clearer idea of a suitable size and shape, mark out the ground with pegs, or lay a hose pipe in the size and shape desired.

Materials

Pools may be constructed using flexible or pre-formed rigid or semi-rigid liners, or mass concrete. The use of flexible liners is now the most popular and cheapest system, but care should be exercised in selecting and installing the appropriate lining material.

Water features can add beauty and interest to any garden. **Above left** An informal cascade and pool. **Right** A rectangular pool enclosed by a narrow border.

It is worth while considering carefully the types of flexible liner available, as buying one of the least expensive forms may prove to be false economy.

Heavy-gauge polythene, with a minimum thickness of 150 micron (600 gauge), is the cheapest but least suitable lining material for, even when used in double thickness, it is not very durable and lacks elasticity. PVC is stronger and more durable and elastic than polythene. It is available in plain, laminated, and nylon-reinforced forms – each progressively stronger and more durable. It comes in various colours, and some liners are stone brown on one side and blue on the other, giving you the choice.

Butyl rubber is regarded as the most useful lining material of all, since it has outstanding durability and can stretch the most easily to conform with the contours of the pool. It is also, however, the most expensive of lining materials. It is most widely available in black or dark grey, but recently a stone-coloured version has been introduced.

Pre-formed pools are available in either semi-rigid plastic or rigid glass-fibre, and most of them are made in irregular shapes. They are more expensive than flexible liners, but are easier to install and less liable to leak. Handymen familiar with glass-fibre construction can make their own pre-formed pools to exactly the required shape and size.

A concrete pool is more difficult and laborious to build, and there is no guarantee that it will not eventually leak unless it is constructed with particular care. It is less easy to construct in informal shapes.

Construction with liners

Before you begin building work, decide on an appropriate shape and size, marking out the site with hose or rope. The area of liner needed will be the maximum length plus twice the depth multiplied by the maximum width plus twice the depth. It is advisable, however, to allow a little more all round to give sufficient margin for overlap at the edges.

If the pool is to be set into a lawn, remove turf 50 to 60 mm (2 to $2\frac{1}{2}$ in) thick (you can use it for extending the lawn elsewhere or for repairing worn or patchy areas). The area removed

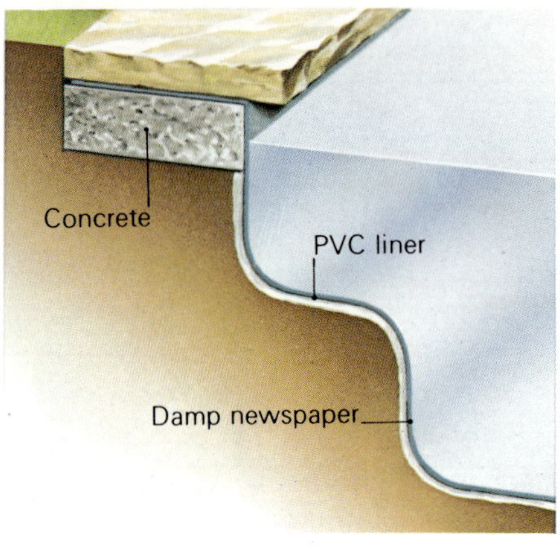

Constructing an irregularly shaped pool using a PVC lining material. **Top** After digging out the hole, check that the top is level all round. **Above** After filling with water, trim off the waste lining material. **Left** Cross-section of pool. The base of the hole should be covered by a thin layer of compacted sand, and the sides with several layers of damp newspaper, before the lining material is installed. The edges of this pool have been strengthened by laying a concrete foundation for the outer edge of the liner to rest on. **Right above** The perimeter of the pool is finished off by bedding coping stones into mortar laid over the liner.

should correspond to the shape of the pool plus the width of the paving stones that will be set around the pool edge. Drive in four pegs at the extremities of the site, and level them off exactly using a straight edge and spirit level. This will give you a better chance of digging out a hole with a level top. Excavate the site to about 230 mm (9 in) depth, sloping the sides inwards by about 75 mm (3 in) for every 230 mm (9 in) depth. This will help to reduce the likelihood of soil subsidence during construction, and will save damage in freezing conditions.

Now dig out the rest of the hole to about 230 to 300 mm (9 to 12 in) deep, again with sloping sides, leaving a 230 mm (9 in) wide planting shelf all round. Remove any sharp projections and smooth over the excavation. Lay a 25 mm (1 in) layer of compacted sand in the bottom and line the sloping sides and shelf with sheets of damp newspaper or old carpet. Carefully unfold and place the liner squarely across the hole, and weight the edges with plenty of brick, blocks, or slabs spaced regularly all the way round. Leave a slight sag in the middle. The liner should if possible be laid in warm weather, when it will stretch more readily and fit more exactly the contours of the hole.

Begin filling the pool slowly with a hose. The liner will gradually sink, partly as a result of stretching and partly by your easing the weights at intervals, until it fits snugly in the excavation. Try to smooth out wrinkles as they occur, although most should have disappeared by the time the pool is full of water.

When the pool is full trim off the waste liner material, leaving about 200 mm (8 in) around the edge for fixing down. In corners and tight bends bunched sheeting must be folded over neatly to hide the surplus; never cut out segments of spare material, as this will almost certainly cause the liner to tear later on.

Pool edges are finished off by bedding coping stones into mortar on top of the folded-over liner. The stones should overlap the pool edge by 30 to 45 mm ($1\frac{1}{4}$ to $1\frac{3}{4}$ in); make sure that

Left An irregularly shaped pool and other water features can look especially effective in association with a rock garden, as here.

they are set firmly, without any tendency to rock. A more substantial edge can be made by providing a concrete foundation for the stones. Dig out a 100 × 300 mm (4 × 12 in) strip all around the pool before installing the liner. Pour a mix of 1:2:4 concrete into the excavated strip and pull the liner tight over the concrete. Fix the slabs directly on top.

Prefabricated pools

Rigid liners are easy to install. Dig a hole about 100 mm (4 in) larger all round than required, then place a compacted layer of sand in the bottom. Place the pool temporarily in position to check that the hole is the right depth, and with the aid of a spirit level and straight edge ensure that the pool edges are perfectly level all round, adjusting the sand bed if necessary.

Once you are satisfied that the pool is level, pack soil tightly around the base section. Be especially careful when doing this to ensure that there are no sharp objects in the soil likely to puncture the liner (the cheaper, semi-rigid types are easily holed in this way). When the lower section of the liner is fixed you may, if you wish, half fill the pool with water. This will help to keep the liner steady while you are filling in the rest of the soil, which should be well compacted. Complete the job by installing coping stones around the edges as described previously.

Making glass-fibre pools

Any shape may be created using glass-fibre mat and polyester resin, but unless you are experienced in using glass fibre you will probably find the experience a little frustrating and difficult. Liners can be made in situ in the excavated hole or formed externally over a mould. The general principles are that the mould, lined usually with polythene, is covered with at least three layers of glass-fibre mat set into resin. Each layer must be set while the last one is still wet, hence sufficient materials must be available to complete the job in one session. The inside layer of resin may be coloured if desired.

Concrete ornamental pools

Although informal shapes are possible, it is much easier to stick to a regularly shaped, formal concrete pool. The main points to remember are that the wall

Constructing a concrete pool. **Below** After digging out the hole, the base is given a foundation of well-rammed and blinded hardcore, in this case overlain by wire-netting reinforcement. **Bottom** After the floor has been laid, reinforcement is positioned around the sloping sides. **Right above** The shuttering for the concrete sides is fixed in position and checked for levels. **Right below** The completed pool, with brick coping and shelf plants, integrated effectively with the pre-cast paving slabs of a patio.

thickness should be not less than 100 mm (4 in), and that the base and sides should be cast in one operation to lessen the risk of junction cracks, which can occur when fresh concrete abuts old. The chance of damage by frost will be greatly reduced if you slope the pool sides by 20 degrees from the vertical (more if possible); this will also reduce the need for shuttering.

Before you begin concreting lay a foundation of 75 to 100 mm (3 to 4 in) of hardcore, rammed down and blinded with damp sand. The concrete should be a conventional 1:2:4 mix containing a proprietary waterproofing additive. Lay the floor first, then the sloping sides. The less steep the slope and the stiffer the concrete, the easier it will be to do this. However, if the concrete tends to sag you will need to use shuttering, which can be wedged in position with struts across the pool. Ensure that the concrete is thoroughly compacted and that a uniform thickness is maintained. As an insurance against the possibility of cracking it may be worth embedding wire netting into the concrete as work proceeds.

Once the concrete has set fill the pool with water to assist the curing (strengthening process). Do not worry if the water level falls at this stage: concrete can absorb a certain amount of water. After a couple of days, drain the pool and allow the concrete to harden for about 4 days. Then apply a 25 mm (1 in) rendering layer of 1:3 cement/soft sand containing the recommended quantity of waterproofing additive; the bond between the two layers can be improved by brushing a dilute solution of PVA adhesive onto the concrete before applying the rendering. The edging slabs can now be laid; they should overlap the edges of the concrete by 25 to 37 mm (1 to 1½ in).

Before stocking with plants or fish you will have to 'condition' the pool because new concrete will make the water alkaline. The best way to do this is to apply one of the proprietary sealing compounds, which will not only neutralize the free lime but also improve the impermeability of the concrete by glazing its surface. The pond can usually be stocked within a couple of days. If you cannot obtain one of these compounds, the best thing to do is to fill the pool with water, let it stand for a few days, then drain and scrub the pool surface thoroughly. You will need to do this two or three times at least, after which it should be safe. Even then, however, it is best to stock with only a few fish at first to see whether they remain healthy.

Leaks in concrete pools can be repaired either by using one of the sealing compounds or by installing a flexible liner. Always fill cracks wider than 10 mm (⅜ in) with mortar before adopting either repair technique.

Fountains

Fountains not only provide a vertical dimension to pools but focus interest in the water garden and create a feeling of coolness and relaxation on a hot summer's day. A useful side effect is that the spray helps to oxygenate the water; this is particularly beneficial in hot, dry weather, when the rate of evaporation is high and pond fish tend to suffer from oxygen starvation.

Design

The most important general consideration is that of scale. A large, powerful fountain in a small pool not only looks somewhat absurd but is likely to spray water over the surrounding area of garden, especially when the spray is caught by gusts of wind; a tiny fountain in a large pool looks mean. Always circulate the water in the pool. This is especially important in a fish pond: water brought in from an outside source will upset the natural balance in the pool and will most probably kill the fishes.

Pumps

Two types of pump may be used. The simplest and cheapest is the mains-operated submersible type, which comprises a simple motor-driven centrifugal pump with a plastic impeller. A strainer is fitted to the inlet to prevent debris being drawn into the pump, and the outlet delivers either to a jet fixed on it or to a remote jet via an extension hose. The other type of pump, usually applicable to larger fountains, is an external (surface) type which is housed in a suitable enclosure by the side of the pool. This type draws water from the pool by a suction hose and then delivers it by hose to the sprayhead.

A mains-operated submersible pump of reputable make is perfectly safe. The waterproof flex can be led out of the pool conveniently hidden from view, and will need to be connected to the supply lead with a proprietary *waterproof* connector. For the ultra-cautious a 24-volt submersible, low-voltage pump unit can be used; this employs a transformer which is housed in a dry place in a convenient shed or garage and can easily be connected to the mains supply.

Fountain nozzles

The size and pattern of spray is determined largely by the capacity of the pump and the friction loss inevitable in long, small-bore hoses. Some retailers operate a pump-exchange scheme whereby a pump of inappropriate power may be exchanged for a more suitable model within a week of original purchase. Most pumps are, however, provided with a means of adjustment on the outlet (nozzle) side, allowing you to find the optimum flow and pressure for your needs. Nozzles should always be positioned just above the water surface. If you buy a submersible pump you will need to provide it with a support to keep the nozzle at the correct height.

There is, incidentally, a wide range of nozzles available, giving different spray patterns. One of the most ambitious displays is the automatic 'water-ballet' fountain, which provides 12 spray patterns.

Left Fountains make an attractive centrepiece of a garden pool. The most important design consideration is to ensure that the spray is neither too large nor too small for the pool.

Lighting

Proprietary garden-lighting kits are available in mains or low-voltage form, and as long as they are used with discretion can add considerable interest to many water features after dark. The most popular type is the above-ground spot or flood, which is normally fixed to the ground with a spike; or it can be attached to a nearby tree or pergola. Underwater lamps can in fact be installed so that they float on the surface, or they can be fully submerged. Both types are available with lenses in a variety of different colours.

It is absolutely vital that only reliable, purpose-designed lamps are used, and that the lead is joined with waterproof connectors to an outdoor supply line complying with the wiring regulations published by the Institution of Electrical Engineers.

Left Underwater lighting can be used to illuminate fountains with dramatic effect. Use only purpose-made lamps and electrical lines with waterproof connectors.

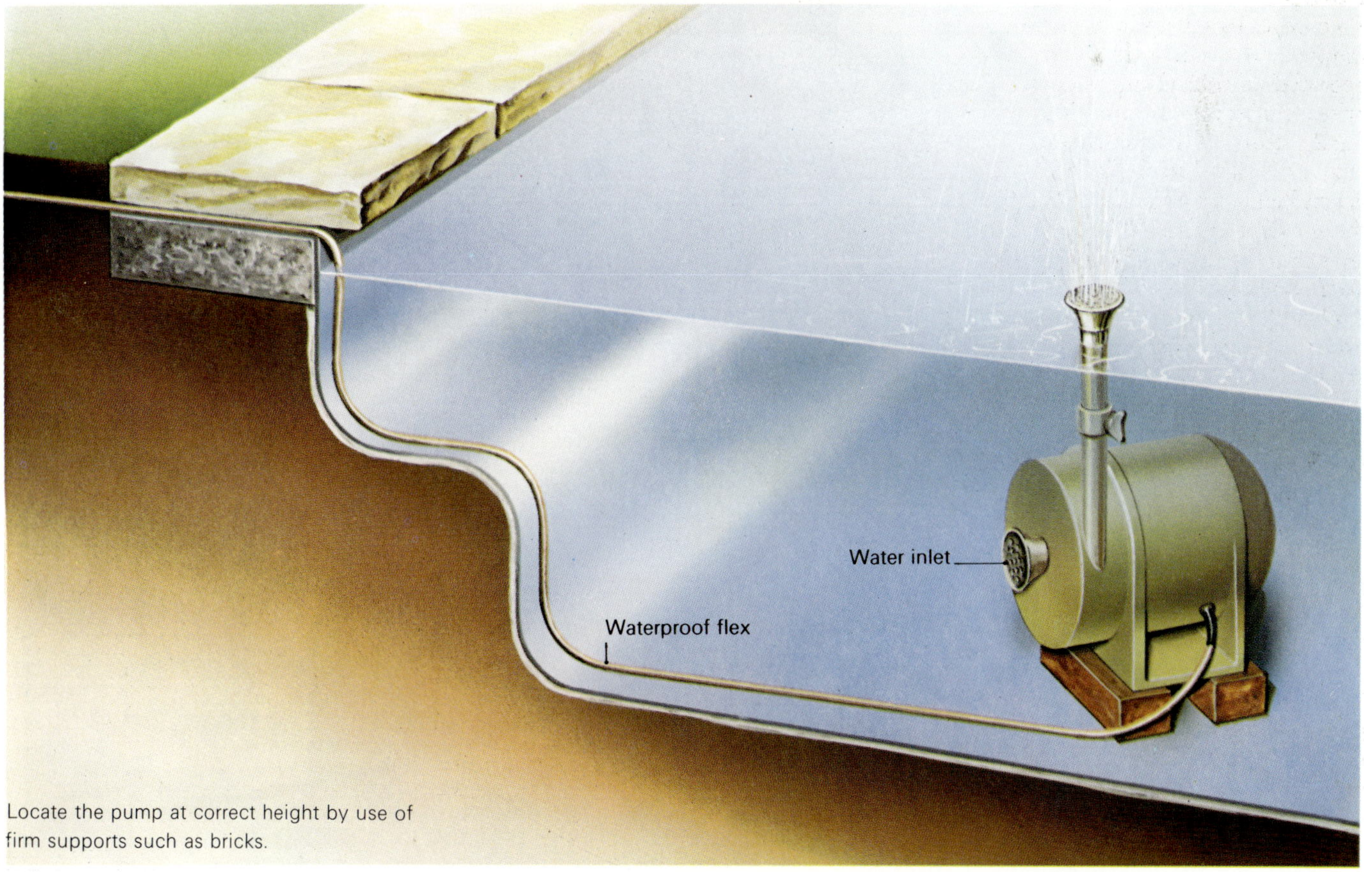

Locate the pump at correct height by use of firm supports such as bricks.

Waterfalls

Waterfalls can be built using a combination of rock, flexible liner, and concrete, or they can be bought in the form of pre-cast synthetic mouldings. The former are generally preferable and certainly give a more natural effect.

The basic principle is to build a series of small tiered pools at least 75 mm (3 in) deep, which are made to overflow as sheets of water, from one to the next, down a slope when the circulation pump is working. The design, however, should if possible be attractive even when the pump is off. The best effect is achieved when the pools form part of a rock garden set on a natural incline, the water finally issuing, perhaps, into a larger, informal pool at the foot of the slope. On a flat site, contours can be created by the soil excavated from the pool.

The general problem, then, is to build a series of small, sealed pools – three or four are quite enough for a small garden – into the slope and thickly set around with rocks. The front edge of each pool should have a perfectly flat ledge, preferably a piece of flat natural stone, over which the water should spill clear of the vertical fall beneath it.

The most difficult part of the construction is sealing the gaps between pools. This can be achieved by overlapping the front edge of the flexible lining sheet of the top pool over the back edge of the lining sheet of the next, lower pool, and bedding them under the lip stone. Alternatively, if you dislike the idea of having visible lining sheets, an adequate seal can be achieved by using a combination of stone and concrete (the latter containing a waterproofing additive).

Below Building a waterfall. Overlapping liners and flat stone at the front of each pool should rest on a firm foundation, preferably of concrete. The pump hose and cable can be buried or concealed by rocks. **Opposite page** A waterfall in a rock garden. Note that the descent of the falls is staggered rather than in a straight line.

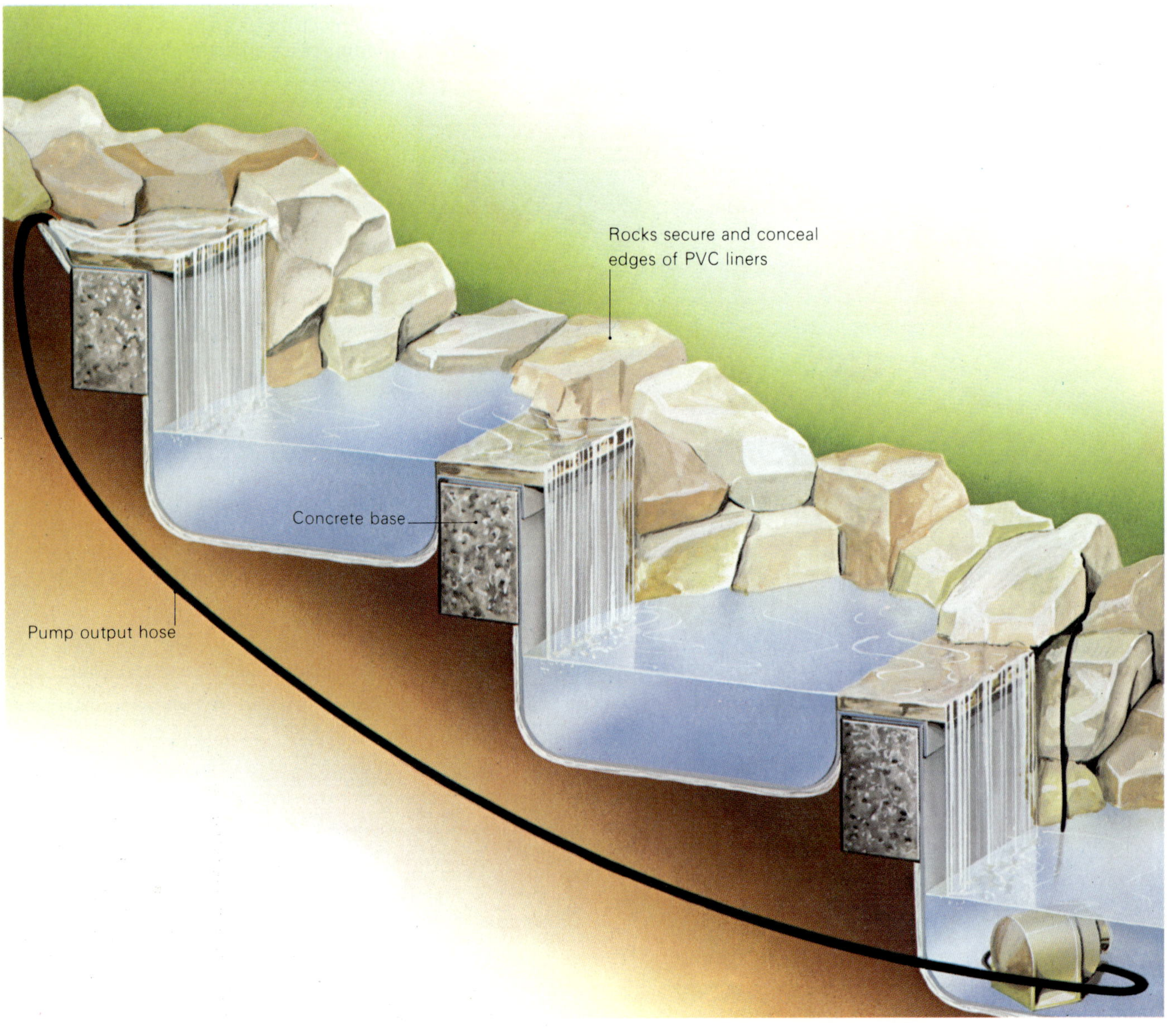

Water flow can be sustained either by means of a separate pump or by using a fountain pump with a second outlet (submersible and surface types are both suitable). The hose supply should be at least 20 mm ($\frac{3}{4}$ in) in diameter to minimise friction; and bear in mind that, with a combined pump, the higher the lift and the longer the second-outlet hose, the smaller will be the fountain spray.

Paddling pools

Paddling pools are great fun for young children – but they are used only in the summer, and even then only for a few years. By all means build one, but think in terms of a design that can be converted into, say, a sand pit.

A permanent structure of this kind can be built in much the same way as the ornamental pools already described. The main additional problem is that the paddling-pool water gets very dirty, so you need to plan for the easy draining and disposal of water. You can either install a drain plug and drainage system, or you can build the pool on ground higher than the surrounding area, so that the water can be syphoned out with a hose. Another alternative, of course, is to pump the water out; small and reasonably inexpensive pumps are available that can be fitted to an electric drill.

The other approach to the paddling pool idea is to build a temporary, above-ground structure. These are easy to erect and dismantle, take up little space, and are indeed most families' answer to the problem. Various kits are on the market that use a basic circular or rectangular framework containing a flexible plastic liner. But you can make your own paddling pool by cutting a 2.4 × 1.2 m (8 × 4 ft) sheet of 3 mm ($\frac{1}{8}$ in) thick, oil-tempered hardboard into three 2.4 m × 400 mm (8 ft × 16 in) strips. Join the sheet ends, so forming them into a circle, by sandwiching them between 100 × 12 mm (4 × $\frac{1}{2}$ in) wooden strips using brass set screws and nuts. Line the container with 300 micron (1,000 gauge) polythene. The liner can be fixed to the top edge of the hardboard surround by making a lengthwise slit in a length of polythene tube, 25 mm (1 in) in diameter, and pushing the slit edge over the hardboard to hold the liner in place.

Outdoor water supplies

In a well-stocked garden, whether large or small, a conveniently sited outdoor watering system is a boon, especially in the summer.

Rainwater

Although most gardeners rely on mains water applied by watering can, hose, or sprinkler, do not forget the possibili-

Right Rigid-plastic water butt fitted with tap and an overflow to a downpipe. **Below** Building a temporary paddling pool: 1 the 2.4 × 1.2 m (8 × 4 ft) sheet of hardboard divided lengthwise into three pieces; 2 the pieces are joined with wooden strips and brass screws and nuts; 3 the hardboard circle; 4 split polythene tubing clamps the liner over the hardboard rim.

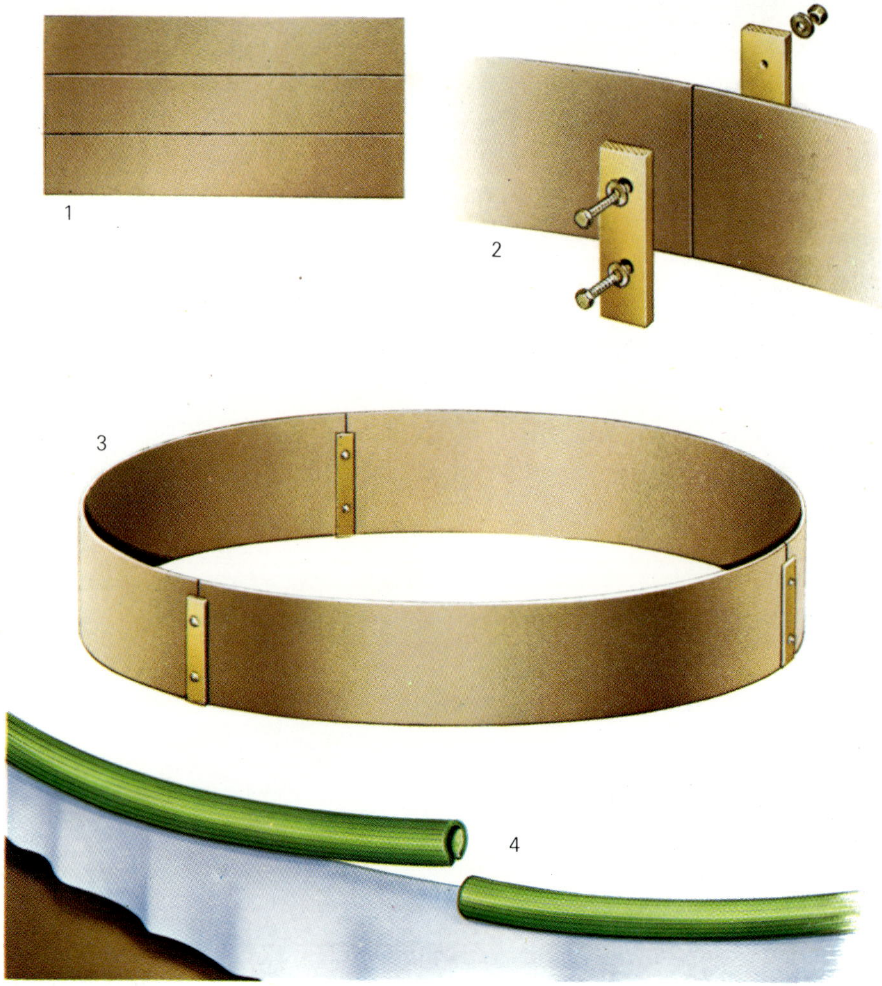

ties of using rainwater collected from the roof. The attraction is that such water has not passed through limestone strata (which render it hard), so it is ideal for watering lime-hating plants such as heaths and rhododendrons. The most convenient form of storage is a water butt, the cheapest models today being of the rigid-plastic type. It is worth choosing a large one – say, 230 l (50 gal) – fitted with a tap and a lid. The lid not only helps to prevent green algae forming and leaves and other debris from falling in, but also deters mosquitoes from breeding on the water surface. Set the butt clear of the ground so that it will be easy to fill watering cans from the tap at the bottom.

The butt is normally supplied from a rainwater downpipe, and should have an overflow to a drain.

Mains water piping

Owing to the amount of water used in the average garden, you will almost certainly need a mains supply from an outside tap as well as a water butt. (The disasters that almost invariably occur when one runs a garden hose from the kitchen tap are too familiar to need mentioning in detail here.) Before installing an outside tap it is advisable to notify your regional water authority. There will probably be no extra charge if you merely use a hand-held hose for watering; but you may have to pay a licence fee if you intend to use non-hand-held sprinklers.

The piping used inside homes today is mainly copper, although galvanized steel is also employed. To fit an extension off the latter type is often quite a complicated business, and unless you have had experience of thread cutting and can get hold of the necessary equipment, you would be well advised to leave this job to a professional plumber. On the other hand, working with copper pipe is quite straightforward, even for the amateur.

The usual sizes of copper piping found in the home are of 15 and 22 mm ($\frac{5}{8}$ and $\frac{7}{8}$ in) outside diameter, these metric sizes having been used exclusively since the early 1970s. 15 mm tube is for most practical purposes of virtually the same size as the old $\frac{1}{2}$ in (internal diameter) tube, but for the 22 mm tube there is no older equivalent and special adaptors are needed to join it to the old $\frac{3}{4}$ in (internal diameter) tube.

The fittings, such as elbows and T's, for copper pipe are of two types: compression joints and soldered joints. The former are the more expensive, but can be easily fixed using two spanners. The soldered joints are either plain ('end-feed') fittings to which solder must be applied; or capillary ('pre-soldered'), in which a ring of solder flows around the pipe when heat is applied.

To form a compression joint, cut the pipe off to the required lengths and carefully remove burr from around the ends with a file. Now slide all the nuts and rings onto the pipe lengths and push them into the fitting. You will find it helpful to smear a little jointing compound around the pipe before screwing up the nuts. Use another spanner, or mole grips, to hold the body of the fitting while the nut is tightened. The nut pushes the ring into the funnel shape of the fitting, and the soft copper or brass ring bites into the pipe and makes a water seal. There is usually no need to tighten the nut more than one quarter or one third of a turn after it is hand tight.

Soldered joints require the use of a blowlamp and take a little longer, although the fittings cost less. When the pipe has been cut and the burr removed, carefully clean about 25 mm (1 in) of the pipe ends and the inside of the fittings with steel wool. Apply soldering flux to the cleaned surfaces and push the pipe into the fitting. With a capillary-type fitting, heat with a blowlamp until a complete ring of solder is visible all around the ends of the fitting. Run in more solder if needed. All the junctions must be soldered in one operation. Such joints are normally soldered on site, with pipes clipped to

Making joints in copper piping. The compression joint (upper drawing) uses a set of nuts and rings. As the nuts are tightened the rings make a seal. In the capillary solder joint (lower drawing) the pipes are slid into opposite ends of a larger-diameter fitting and past two rings of solder which make a seal when heated with a blowlamp.

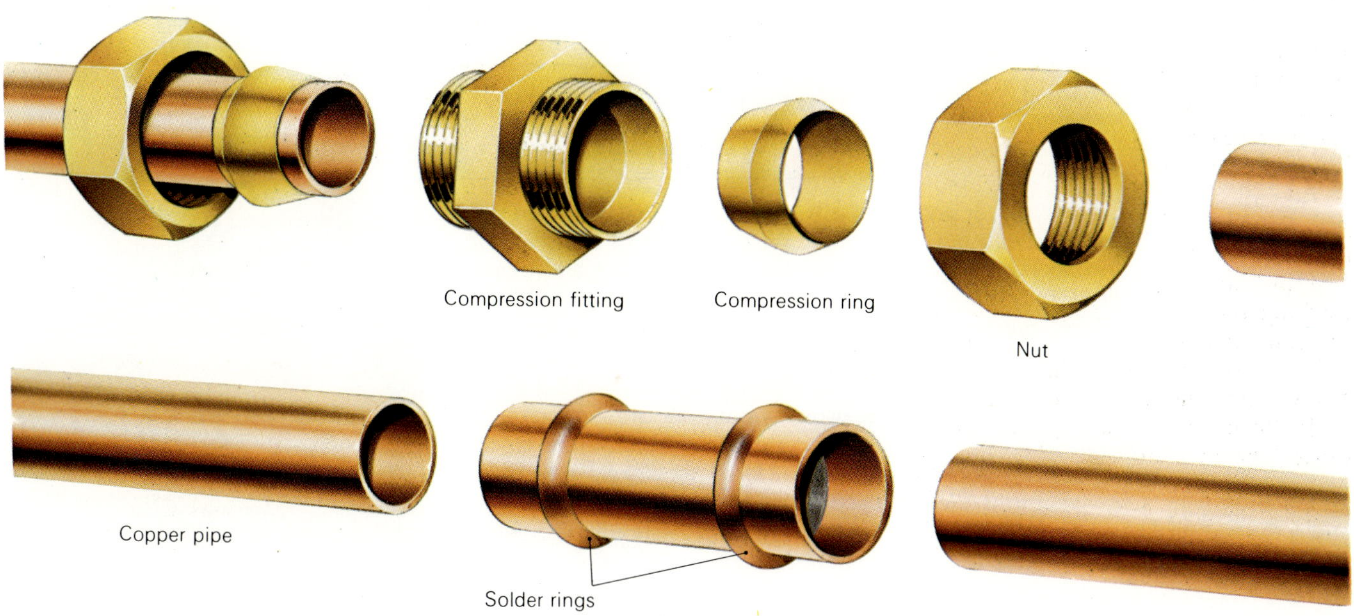

the wall, so put soft asbestos sheeting behind the joint to protect the wall.

The time and expense of using elbow fittings with copper tube can sometimes be saved by bending the tube into a fairly gentle curve. Insert a pipe-bending spring, then bend the tube around the curve of your thigh.

PLASTIC TUBE Semi-rigid polythene tube, such as 'Alkathene', is very commonly used as cold-water piping outside the house. It is relatively cheap, available in long lengths, immensely durable, corrosion-free, and can be formed into gentle bends without the need for fittings. Another advantage is that it has a measure of elasticity, so that if the water freezes the tube rarely bursts. This type of tube is therefore ideal for supplying a stand pipe at a convenient spot in the garden.

The tube should be buried at a depth of about 600 mm (2 ft). If you need to bend it around some obstruction, heat that section of pipe in hand-hot water for 5 minutes. Fittings used with this tube are of the compression type, with a copper insert pushed into the ends of each tube so that they will not collapse when the nuts are tightened. (Incidentally, fittings are available to enable you to join polythene tube to copper piping.)

Fitting an outside tap

Unless you have a larger-than-average garden it will probably be most convenient to fit the tap on the outside wall of the house. The easiest way to do this is to branch off just above the main stop tap, where the rising mains enters the house. A drain valve is usually associated with this stop tap, so that when the supply is turned off the piping system can be drained down before a section of pipe is cut out to take a T-joint.

Use 15 mm ($\frac{5}{8}$ in) diameter copper tube for the branch line, and fit a new stop tap to enable you to isolate the outside tap in winter. Continue the pipe run to the outside of the house. The pipe should emerge at a higher level than the intended tap, so that it will be easy to drain down the outside section of pipe in the winter.

The pipe ends in a wall-plate elbow, which should be screwed into drilled and plugged holes using galvanized screws. Once the elbow is fixed, the outside tap with hose-bib fitting is screwed into the elbow using PTFE sealing tape wrapped around the threads.

If you need a second, free-standing tap, use a wall-plate tee instead of the wall-plate elbow. From there you can continue the remaining run of piping in polythene tube.

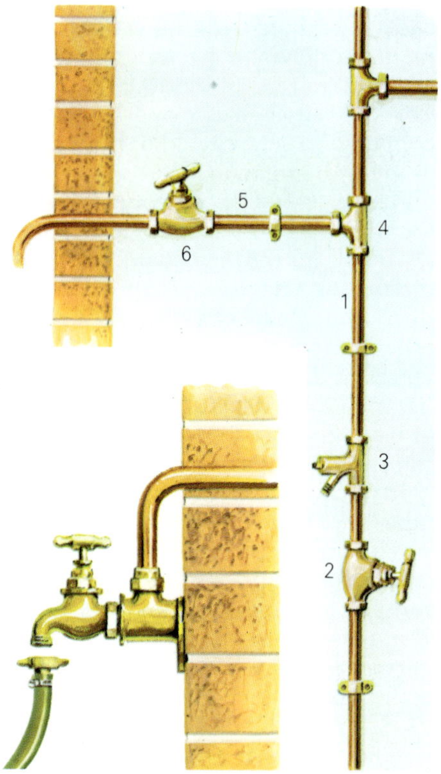

Plumbing for an outdoor tap: 1 Rising main; 2 Main stopcock; 3 Draincock; 4 T-joint; 5 Branch through house wall to outdoor tap; 6 New stopcock. Enlarged drawing at left shows outside pipe to wall-plate elbow (screwed to wall) and new tap.

Garden watering equipment

Garden hose, usually of 12 mm ($\frac{1}{2}$ in) nominal bore, is made of PVC in one, two, or three layers. The three-layer forms are reinforced with nylon or rayon braid between the layers, and some of the two-layer versions are also reinforced. When selecting a hose the primary considerations (apart from cost) should be how easy it is to roll and unroll in all weathers, how prone it is to kinking, and how great is its bursting strength. Reinforced hoses are better on all counts.

For a neat, tidy, and safe garden, hoses should be wound onto a reel. Many reels are of the through-feed type, enabling you to unwind as much of the hose off the reel as you need and to connect a short length of hose from the tap to the reel inlet. Some are suitable for wall mounting near the tap. Fittings are available for attaching the hose to a tap or for joining two or more hoses together.

Hand-held watering rose with fine spray.

Irrigation water must be broken into fairly fine droplets and applied evenly, otherwise plants can be damaged and the soil can cap easily; so garden hoses need some form of spray attachment. Three types of hand-held sprayers are commonly used, two of which – the spray-nozzle type and the gun type – can be adjusted to form fine or coarse spray; the watering-rose type has no adjustment.

More convenient – but also consi-

Below Static sprinkler rotated by water pressure. **Right** Oscillating sprinkler.

derably more expensive – than hand-held sprayers are water sprinklers, which are capable of applying a spray over large areas. There are five types.

Static sprinklers are the simplest, most models having no moving parts. They are usually fitted with a spike for fixing them to the ground. It is essential to fit the spike perfectly upright, otherwise the water-distribution pattern will be distorted.

Rotating sprinklers give a fairly good uniformity of cover. Most have two or three arms that rotate freely about a central column. Water travels up the column and out of small holes in the ends of the arms: the rotating action is caused by the water pressure. Some models have adjustment for fineness of spray, others for the angle of trajectory.

Oscillating sprinklers have a flat or curved spray bar with small holes in the upper portion from which the water issues. A small water-driven motor and gearbox causes the spraybar to oscillate from side to side. Most have a means of setting the area to be sprayed. There is no adjustment for fineness, and usually the uniformity of cover is inferior to that of some of the other types.

Sprinkler hoses are flattened hosepipes with holes along the topside – but again the uniformity of cover is poor.

The most expensive type of all is the travelling sprinkler. It is especially useful for watering large lawns because it does away with the need to move the watering system from place to place. Most types work by using a water-driven winch either to wind in a steel tape previously paid out or to haul in the hose onto a reel.

Self-powered travelling sprinkler – useful for watering a large expanse of lawn.

8 Timber Features

THERE are many useful wooden garden structures that you can make yourself, including pergolas and arches; frames, and a variety of garden furniture.

Wood is strong and readily workable, but it is important that it is in the right condition when you buy it. The growing tree contains a very large amount of moisture, and, when it is felled, this water has to be removed. Normally the tree is cut up into boards, which are then stacked with spacers between them in open-sided sheds to season. As the water evaporates the timber shrinks a little and becomes lighter and stronger. Seasoned timber is more resistant to decay, and paint will adhere to it more readily. It is important to buy only well-seasoned timber. If you make a structure from timber that is still 'green', shrinkage will cause the joints to open up, and this will not only weaken them but allow rain water to penetrate – and this can lead to speedy rotting of the wood.

Types of timber

There are three categories of timber available: softwoods, hardwoods, and man-made boards.

SOFTWOOD, which is from coniferous trees with needle-like leaves, is the most readily available and least expensive. The commonest forms are red and white deal. Red deal is red Baltic pine or Scots pine; if treated with preservative it is suitable for outdoor use, but it tends to be rather knotty. White deal (spruce) is not suitable for outdoor use. Douglas fir and hemlock are both relatively knot-free softwoods and can be used outdoors if they are treated with a preservative. The most durable softwoods for garden structures are larch and western red cedar. Larch is ideal for many purposes but needs to be preserved. Western red cedar, however, contains its own preservative oils, giving it outstanding durability and an attractive finish when used, say, for cladding a garden shed; however, it needs to be sealed with a varnish to prevent the natural oils from leaching out and turning the wood grey. Although durable, western red cedar is less strong than some other softwoods and is also more expensive.

HARDWOODS come from broad-leaved deciduous trees; in general they cost a great deal more than softwoods, but they are much more durable. There are two main types: native British hardwoods and African hardwoods. Of the first type, beech is the most commonly used, but elm and oak are the most suitable for garden structures. Owing to the number of trees felled as a consequence of Dutch elm disease, elm is at present one of the cheapest hardwoods. It is very resistant to splitting and makes excellent garden seats and tables. Oak is heavy, very expensive, but immensely strong and durable, and garden furniture and fence posts made from it should last a lifetime. The use of oak calls for competence in the forming of woodworking joints because oak contains tannic acid, which corrodes steel fittings such as nails and screws.

Among the African hardwoods, iroko, which has similar properties and appearance to teak but is about half the price, is ideal for garden furniture, and it requires no preservative.

MAN-MADE BOARDS Plywood and hardboard are suitable for outdoor use, but only in their exterior grades. The rather expensive marine ply or WBP plywood consists of thin layers of wood glued together with weather- and boiling-proof glue, with the grain in each layer running at right angles to those above and below it. This gives it great stiffness. Oil-tempered hardboard is made of wood pulp mixed with waterproof glue hot-pressed into sheets. It is quite cheap but not very strong.

Buying timber

Most timber is sold in lengths that are multiples of 300 mm ($11\frac{3}{4}$ in) and in sections from about 25 × 25 mm (1 × 1 in) upwards. This refers to sawn timber; 'planed-all-round' (PAR) timber is about 3 mm ($\frac{1}{8}$ in) less in width and thickness and costs more. Avoid buying timber with defects such as 'dead' knots, which will usually fall out, and shakes (splits) unless they are at the ends and can be cut off. Natural boarding is generally available in two main profiles: shiplap, which is used horizontally for cladding, and tongue-and-groove, which is used vertically. The commonest sizes are 20 × 100 mm ($\frac{3}{4}$ × 4 in), 25 × 125 mm (1 × 5 in), and 25 × 150 mm (1 × 6 in).

Rustic timber furniture, simple to make, looks well in a country garden.

Man-made plywood boards are usually sold as sheets 2440 mm × 1220 mm (8 × 4 ft) in thicknesses ranging from 3 mm ($\frac{1}{8}$ in) to about 25 mm (1 in); tempered hardboard is normally available only in thicknesses of 3.2 mm ($\frac{1}{8}$ in) and 6.4 mm ($\frac{1}{4}$ in).

Timber preservation

All softwoods except western red cedar must be properly preserved for exterior use. For fence panels preservation with creosote is quite adequate, but fence posts should be steeped for several hours in a barrel of creosote which is heated and then allowed to cool. Only by using this method will the creosote be drawn to sufficient depth into the timber to confer long-term protection. Creosoted timber cannot, of course, be painted.

For little extra cost you can buy treated softwoods from the timber merchant; these will have been preserved by one of several proprietary treatment systems, some of which are applied by immersion, others by a vacuum process. Once treated, such timber is protected from decay by fungus or from insect attack for life. Other chemicals can be applied by brush after you have bought the timber; but they do not penetrate so deep, and you will have to repeat the treatment every couple of years or so. Unlike creosoted timber, surfaces treated with these chemicals can be painted once they have dried out thoroughly. Paint on its own will help to protect softwood, but it offers no guarantee that rotting will not ensue.

Technique

From the foregoing, it will be clear that (putting aside the question of cost) it is important that you begin by selecting the type of wood most appropriate for the project you have in mind. Second, choose section sizes that, on the one hand, are sufficiently strong and, on the other hand, are not too bulky. Unless you are a fairly experienced woodworker, the sensible thing to do is to have a good look at some typical designs, either at a garden centre or in a neighbour's garden, and modify them to suit your particular needs.

Mark out and cut joints accurately, then lock them firmly together for strength, neatness, and minimum maintenance, using bracing pieces wherever appropriate. The essence of well designed woodwork joints is that they rely only partly, if at all, on nails or screws for their strength. This applies especially to outdoor woodwork because steel fittings will eventually be destroyed by rust. If, as is probable, you have to use such fittings, supplement the strength of the joints by using wood glues. Above all, make sure that your design prevents rainwater from entering the grain of the wood at timber ends. Moisture will cause distortion of the wood by swelling and will eventually cause it to rot. Some glues, incidentally, offer a certain degree of waterproofing.

FIXING DEVICES There is a wide range of nails and screws available, but you should always use galvanized types for outdoor structures. Nails are cheaper and quicker to use, but should be employed only on joints where the surfaces are trying to slide over each other. By contrast, screws are better where the elements of the joint are tending to pull apart; in any case, they give a stronger fixing than nails, can be removed more readily, and generally give a neater appearance. Nails should be driven in at an angle to the wood surface, and staggered to avoid splitting the grain. If possible use nails that are two or three times as long as the thickness of the uppermost piece of timber. Screws should be set into pilot holes; or, better, preform the hole by using a gimlet. Counter-sink the top of the hole so that the screw head fits flush with the surface of the wood.

Woodworking glues considerably add to the strength of joints if used with other fixing devices. The important thing to remember is to use a type suitable for external use; among the best are those based on urea formaldehyde (PVA woodworking adhesives are suitable only for indoor use.)

WOODWORKING JOINTS Most garden timber projects can be constructed using L or T joints. L, or corner, joints can be made by butting the two members and nailing or screwing them together; both pieces must be cut perfectly square to give a neat waterproof joint. However, it is a fairly weak joint, and working so near the end of the wood may cause splitting. Butt joints can be strengthened by adding some form of timber gusset, or by using metal corner brackets. A better and stronger alternative is a rebated joint. Cut the rebate carefully with a tenon saw and avoid making it deeper than about half the thickness of the timber. Apply glue, and nail the rebated sections together.

There are of course more complex corner joints, such as box and dovetailed types, but their use is not warranted for most outdoor projects, and some of them require special tools.

T joints can be formed in a variety of ways. Where the two members are of the same cross-section the simplest method is a butt joint using nails or screws; if appearance is not important, a pair of steel brackets can simplify the job. A stronger alternative is an overlap joint which is glued and screwed. If necessary the cross rail can be recessed into the side rail.

The T halving joint is made by cutting away both members so that a flush firm fit is achieved when they are mated. On the top face of the side rail mark the width of the cross rail checking with a T square that it is at right angles, and continue the marks down the sides. Use a mortise gauge to score a mark on each side of the side rail to indicate the depth of the recess, which should be equal to half the rail thickness. Using the gauge at the same setting score a mark around the end of the cross rail. At a distance about 12 mm ($\frac{1}{2}$ in) longer than the rail width mark a 'shoulder' line on the cross member. Remove the surplus wood from the cross rail with a tenon saw, keeping to the waste side of the mark. Make two saw cuts where marked in the side rail to the depth indicated. Make another one in the centre of the waste wood; this will make it easier to remove with a wood chisel, working from both sides to achieve a flat true channel. Apply adhesive, then screw or nail the joint together.

To fabricate a T joint where the cross rail joins an upright of larger section, such as in a gate, a mortise and tenon will provide one of the strongest and neatest joints.

The mortise should never be cut wider than one third of the thickness of the upright, otherwise the latter's strength will be impaired. Marking out follows a similar procedure to that for the T halving joint, using a mortise gauge to mark out the width of the

Some typical woodworking joints.

Overlap T joint

Full-lap T joint

T halving joint

Box joint

Through mortise-and-tenon joint

Mortise-and-tenon with wedges

On a rustic timber arch, the bark which will eventually loosen, is best removed before construction.

mortise on the upright and the tenon on the cross rail.

The waste is simply cut from the tenon using a tenon saw, while the mortise is cut out with a mortise chisel and mallet. It is often useful to cut a pair of tapers on the outside vertical faces of the mortise; then tapered wedges can be driven into these 'slots' after adhesive has been applied and the parts mated together. This produces a very firm joint. A peg fixing is another alternative. Drill through the joint, making the hole in the tenon a few millimetres short of that through the mortise. Enter the tenon into the mortise and drive tapered dowelling through the hole; this will draw the tenon up into a very firm joint.

Some typical projects

The following are a few of the many garden structures that the average handyman can make without much difficulty.

Pergolas and arches

These are usually constructed entirely of timber, although brick, stone, or metal uprights can also be used if you prefer it. The timber can be squared or 'rustic'. In the latter case larch poles are best. Leave the bark on only if the larch has been felled during the winter; otherwise the bark will eventually fall off. It is probably better to remove it with a knife or spoke shave, and to apply varnish or creosote to the underlying surface. Only butt joints are possible with rustic poles, and both joint faces must be squared before they are nailed together.

Although slim poles may look better when the pergola or arch is bare, be fairly generous with the thickness as the structure may eventually have to bear a considerable weight of foliage. Uprights should be treated like fence posts (*see* Chapter 3); they must be well preserved and set firmly at least 450 mm (18 in) in the ground.

A pergola can transform a dull path into an interesting open tunnel clothed, perhaps, in fragrant and colourful clim-

Left Pergola with crossrails braced with diagonal struts. Below Pergola upright set in a brick and concrete foundation.

bers. It is important that it is made not too narrow: make it about as wide as it is high. It is constructed of a series of three basic members: the uprights, cross rails, and side members.

Uprights should be spaced no more than 2.4 m (8 ft) apart, and should not be less than 100 mm (4 in) in diameter or square. A variety of possibilities exist for the cross rails, but they should be a minimum of 75 mm (3 in) in diameter or square; a pleasing effect is produced if they extend each side of the uprights, with shaped ends. Some people who prefer a more sturdy appearance use wider but thinner cross rails, such as planking 150 × 25 mm (6 × 1 in). Side members should be about the same size as the cross rails, or a little smaller if you prefer it.

To help climbers clothe the pergola, attach longitudinally a series of laths about 50 × 25 mm (2 × 1 in) in section and spaced about 500 mm (20 in) apart. It is also a good idea to fix wires along the top members.

Arches are constructed in a similar way except that a narrower and slimmer but braced frame will look more attractive. A typical rustic arch can be formed with basic frames consisting of a pair of uprights topped with a headpiece using 75 mm (3 in) diameter poles, and with two 50 mm (2 in) internal braces under the head; the frames are then linked with 50 mm (2 in) struts and braces.

Garden furniture

Most people prefer to buy ready-made garden furniture, but you can save a lot of money if you make it yourself; moreover, it is especially rewarding to make custom-built items – such as a bench around the trunk of a tree – that you may not be able to buy in the size or shape you want. Unless you are experienced in woodwork the best advice is not to be too ambitious and to keep your projects simple in form. Above all, beware that, in ensuring that your seats and chairs are strong and stable, they do not look unattractively bulky. Avoid copying rustic furniture that has wide boards.

A simple garden bench can be constructed using two pieces of pine or hardwood about 200 × 37 mm (8 × 1½ in) nominal size, and no more than 1.2 m (48 in) long. These can be bolted to a pair of painted, mild-steel support frames of 50 × 6 mm (2 × ¼ in) section. A more ambitious garden seat with back can be made using a framework of

Right Easy-to-make timber features. The table with built-in benches is similar in design to that in the drawing below.

Bench seat

Table

Table with built-in benches

nominal 62 × 37 mm ($2\frac{1}{2}$ × $1\frac{1}{2}$ in) section clad with seven rails of 100 × 32 mm (4 × $1\frac{1}{4}$ in) section. With rails of this size the seat can be up to 1.5 m (5 ft) long. Three frames are required. Each pair of legs is joined with a halving joint. Bolts and timber connectors are used for jointing to the top horizontal member. The legs are stiffened with either cross or longitudinal members or both. Before they are screwed to the framework, the cladding rails should have their top edges rounded off.

A special feature can be created of a tree in a lawn or paved area by building a seat around the trunk. It is advisable to use a hardwood, such as iroko, because the seat will often be wettened by damp leaves. Probably the simplest design is triangular rather than circular in plan; it is formed by making up three chair-section frames and linking them with rails for the seat base and back. The size of timber necessary depends, of course, on the girth of the trunk, which determines the span from frame to frame. Usually

Left A rustic seat. **Below** A seat and child's play pit built around a tree.

Above Sturdy, easy-to-build garden chairs.

62×37 mm ($2\frac{1}{2} \times 1\frac{1}{2}$ in) section will be sufficient for the framework and 75×32 mm ($3 \times 1\frac{1}{4}$ in) section for the seat base and back rails. On a lawn it will be necessary to distribute the weight of the legs by setting them on tiles or bricks below the lawn surface.

A garden table suitable for outdoor meals should be large enough to accommodate everyone concerned – yet it should not take up too much space in a small garden. For this reason a table that can be dismantled is likely to be most useful. Make the table top a comfortable height in relation to the chairs being used; anything between 650 and 730 mm (26 and 29 in) will probably be satisfactory. One of the simplest designs consists of a top of 150×37 mm ($6 \times 1\frac{1}{2}$ in) planks, set with a 20 mm ($\frac{3}{4}$ in) gap between each, and supported on two or three leg frames of 62×37 mm ($2\frac{1}{2} \times 1\frac{1}{2}$ in) section. The lower part of each leg frame is braced to the next by means of a central longitudinal member. Slightly more ambitious is a picnic table that includes built in benches. Such tables have the advantage that the benches provide additional longitudinal bracing to the structure as a whole.

Garden frames

A garden frame is at once one of the most easily built and most useful assets of the amateur gardener, whether he has a greenhouse or not. It consists essentially of one or more glazed frames sloping at an angle of 10 degrees or more and covering a small walled enclosure; it should be sited in a sunny spot, with the glass sloping towards the south for the optimum effect. Commonly the frame, or light, is 1.5 m (5 ft) long by 750 mm (2 ft 6 in) wide and glazed with one large sheet of 4 mm (32 oz) glass, but various alternatives are possible using a central glazing bar and perhaps four smaller panes.

The most important first step is to provide yourself with an absolutely flat surface, so that the frame has no built-in warps. To accept the glass a

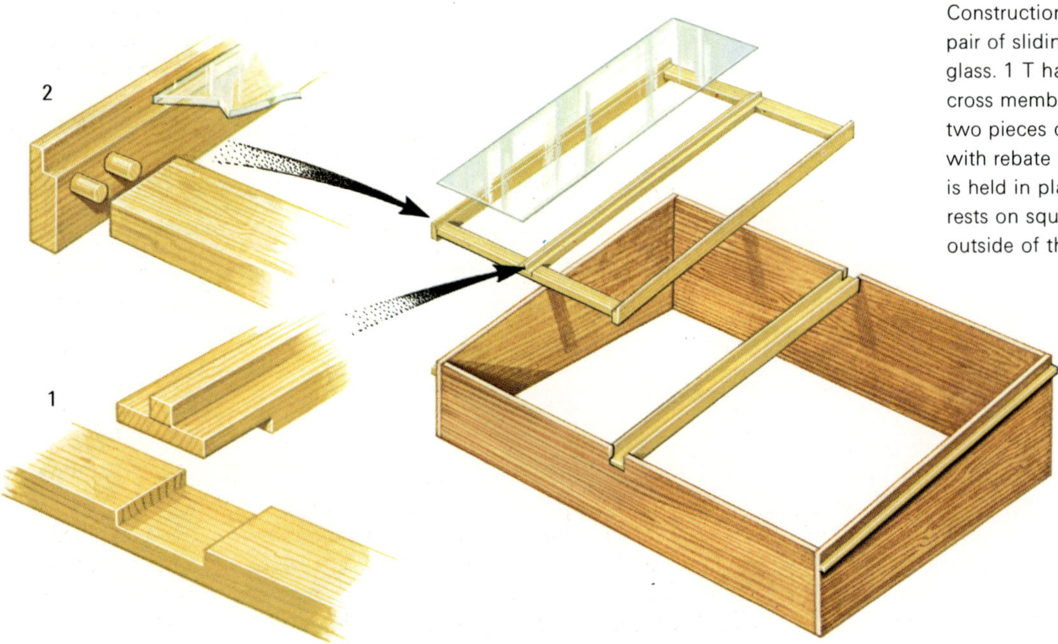

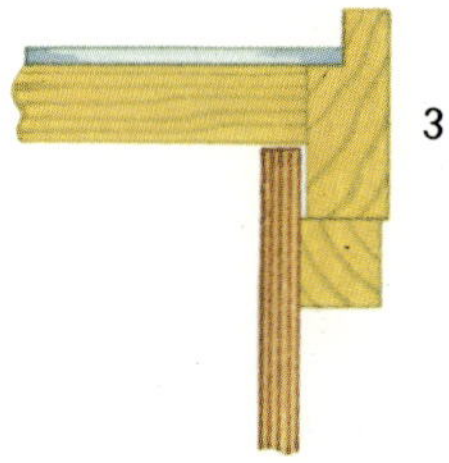

Construction of a garden cold frame with a pair of sliding lights, each with two panes of glass. 1 T halving joint for centre rail and cross member. 2 Butt-corner joint made with two pieces of glued dowelling. 3 Side rail with rebate cut in top edge for pane, which is held in place with glazing sprigs. The rail rests on square-section batten fixed to the outside of the plywood base.

Construction of greenhouse benching. The framework is of 50 × 50 mm (2 × 2 in) section pieces secured with rebated and T halving joints, and with side and diagonal braces to ensure rigidity. The bench top consists of spaced slats of 50 × 22 mm (2 × $\frac{7}{8}$ in) section, and is finished at the front and rear edges with 25 × 25 mm (1 × 1 in) section batten.

groove will need to be cut in the side rails; alternatively, a rebate can be cut in their top edges and the glass held down by glazing sprigs. Use 62 × 37 mm (2$\frac{1}{2}$ × 1$\frac{1}{2}$ in) section pieces laid on edge for the side rails and laid flat for the cross members. Make butt-corner joints and secure each of them with two pieces of glued dowelling rather than nails. To make the frame water-tight extend the side rails about 20 mm ($\frac{3}{4}$ in) below the cross rails, so that the frame edges can be supported on 25 × 25 mm (1 × 1 in) battens on the outside of the enclosure.

The walls can be made of various materials – but remember that, if you use bricks, they will have to be tapered to allow the framelight to slope. A more easily built alternative uses 20 mm ($\frac{3}{4}$ in) exterior-grade ply, cutting the taper for the pair of side panels with one cut from a piece 700 mm × 1.5 m (28 in × 5 ft). The back panel should be about 400 mm (16 in) high and the front one about 300 mm (12 in). Set the walled enclosure on a single layer of bricks laid dry. For a multi-unit frame, intermediate support rails will be needed and should be set flush into the front and back panels. Make up gutter-shaped rails with a pair of 50 × 20 mm (2 × $\frac{3}{4}$ in) laths nailed each side so that the edges of the frame sit snugly and water is drained away. Finish the frame with an undercoat and a top coat of exterior-grade paints. Use the colour of your choice on the outside, but if the interior is painted white it will increase the amount of reflected light within the frame.

Window boxes

These are easy to construct, and when well stocked they can transform both the interior and exterior view. Size will obviously depend on the window, but a box looks best if it is full width and about 150 to 250 mm (6 to 10 in) high. It is essential to fix the box in place, even on flat sills, in order to avoid accidents. On sloping sills the box will need to be constructed with a sloping floor retained in position by screwing the sides to the window reveals. One of the simplest designs uses 12 mm ($\frac{1}{2}$ in) thick exterior-grade plywood panels for the sides and bottom nailed to 32 mm (1$\frac{1}{4}$ in) softwood end members. Remember to drill holes in the bottom panel to allow excess water to drain away.

Greenhouse benching

The design of this equipment will be determined partly by the space available and partly by the weight of pots and seed trays they have to support. The minimum size of framework is 50 × 50 mm (2 × 2 in) section. The bench top should consist of slats of nominal 50 × 22 mm (2 × $\frac{7}{8}$ in) section spaced 12 to 20 mm ($\frac{1}{2}$ to $\frac{3}{4}$ in) apart. The slats should rest on a top framework made of a front and back rail with cross members every 1 m (39 in). Half-lap the legs on to the side rails and brace the legs together near floor level. From this piece run a diagonal brace to the next cross member in the top frame; this will further increase the rigidity of the structure.

Compost bins

Garden waste material can be converted into valuable humus if it is composted in a heap. The best way to achieve this is to build not one compost bin but two or three. One bin can then be used for incoming material and the other(s) for immediately usable compost. Sawn, well-preserved timber can be made up to make open-topped boxes, the size of which will be determined by the amount of waste to be treated. A simple design is to set six 100 × 100 mm (4 × 4 in) section posts into the ground to form the corners of two adjoining bins. The sides can be made from 25 mm (1 in) thick sawn boards. The easiest way to attach the sides is to form vertical grooves on the post sides, using two parallel 32 × 25 mm (1$\frac{1}{4}$ × 1 in) section laths about 32 mm (1$\frac{1}{4}$ in) apart, into which the boards can be slotted one by one. Aeration of the compost will be improved if you set spacers between the boards.

9 The Handyman's Tools

EVEN if you contemplate undertaking only a fraction of the projects outlined in this book, you will find an adequate set of tools to be an excellent investment. There is a vast difference between having the right tool for the job and making do with one that was designed to do something else. Although the prices of the tools you may need for some of these projects are considerable, you can be confident that most, if not all, are cheaper than hiring a skilled craftsman to do the job for you. Savings can often be made by buying tools and equipment secondhand, perhaps at an auction or through advertisements in trade journals.

Make a point of buying good quality tools: if they are to be used frequently they will justify their price in the long run. Do not rush into purchases: examine tools closely to see if they will do all you expect of them.

The following are some of the basic tools that you will need for the projects I have described in the previous chapters of this book.

Garden tools

For groundwork a shovel is needed in addition to a spade and fork. It is particularly useful for mixing mortar and concrete and for spreading hardcore and sand. The typical garden wheelbarrow is unsuitable for moving large quantities of earth, hardcore, and concrete: it is not only too small, but will probably not stand up to the weight of the loads it will be asked to carry. You will almost certainly be able to buy a builder's wheelbarrow secondhand, which you can sell when you have finished with it. Alternatively, you may be able to hire one from a local building contractor.

For measuring, an inexpensive retractable steel tape 3 m (10 ft) long is both convenient and versatile; for longer distances a 10 m (33 ft) cloth tape might be useful. Accuracy in checking levels demands a good spirit level. Select one about 600 mm (2 ft) long with a pair of clearly visible, barrel-shaped vials to indicate both horizontal and vertical surfaces.

When it comes to bricklaying and concreting, 10 l (2 gal) heavy-duty plastic buckets are strongly recommended for measuring materials accurately as well as for carrying mortar and concrete. A 250 mm (10 in) bricklayer's trowel and a smaller pointing trowel form the basis of the tool kit, which should also include a 1 kg (2.2 lb) lump hammer and a bolster chisel for cutting bricks, a length of line and pins, and (for laying concrete) a steel or wooden float.

Basic woodworking techniques require a 550 mm (22 in) general-purpose saw and a 250 to 300 mm (10 to 12 in) tenon saw for cutting joints. You will need a set-square for marking out and a mortise gauge for accuracy in the making of many joints. For fastenings a 400 g (16 oz) claw hammer, pincers, a gimlet, a drill, a countersink, and large and small screwdrivers are tools that should be found in every handyman's toolbox, and 12 mm ($\frac{1}{2}$ in) and 25 mm (1 in) wood chisels and a wooden mallet are needed for all but the simplest joints.

Plumbing with copper or plastic tube does not require special equipment. A junior hacksaw is quite adequate for cutting the tube and a small file is useful to remove burr. For soldered joints a multi-purpose butane blowlamp is the most convenient to use, while spanners are needed for compression joints. To bend copper tube you will need a bending spring.

Other general-purpose tools you will find useful for a wide range of projects include a retractable-bladed knife, a pair of pliers, a plumb bob, a sanding block, a rasp with flat and curved surfaces, and a nail punch.

Special tools

For cutting bricks quickly the professional way, a brick hammer is the answer. A curved pointing tool is particularly useful for pointing between paving slabs. Levelling the surface of a large area of newly laid concrete requires the use of a bull float – a steel float with a wide head on a long handle; but this is something you should be able to hire. To ease the moving of hard ground, particularly if it is engulfed with builders' debris, a builder's pick is a most useful asset, while a crowbar can be useful for loosening large stones and also for moving and setting stones in the rock garden.

Builder's tools: 1 Shovel, 2 Bolster chisel, 3 Club hammer, 4 Spirit level, 5 Steel float, 6 Line pins, 7 Bricklayer's hammer, 8 Line and plumb bob, 9 Pointing trowel, 10 Bricklaying trowel, 11 Steel tape, 12 Cloth tape. A builder's wheelbarrow is another important item.

1
2
3
4
5
6
7
8
9
10
11
12
STANLEY
POWERLOCK

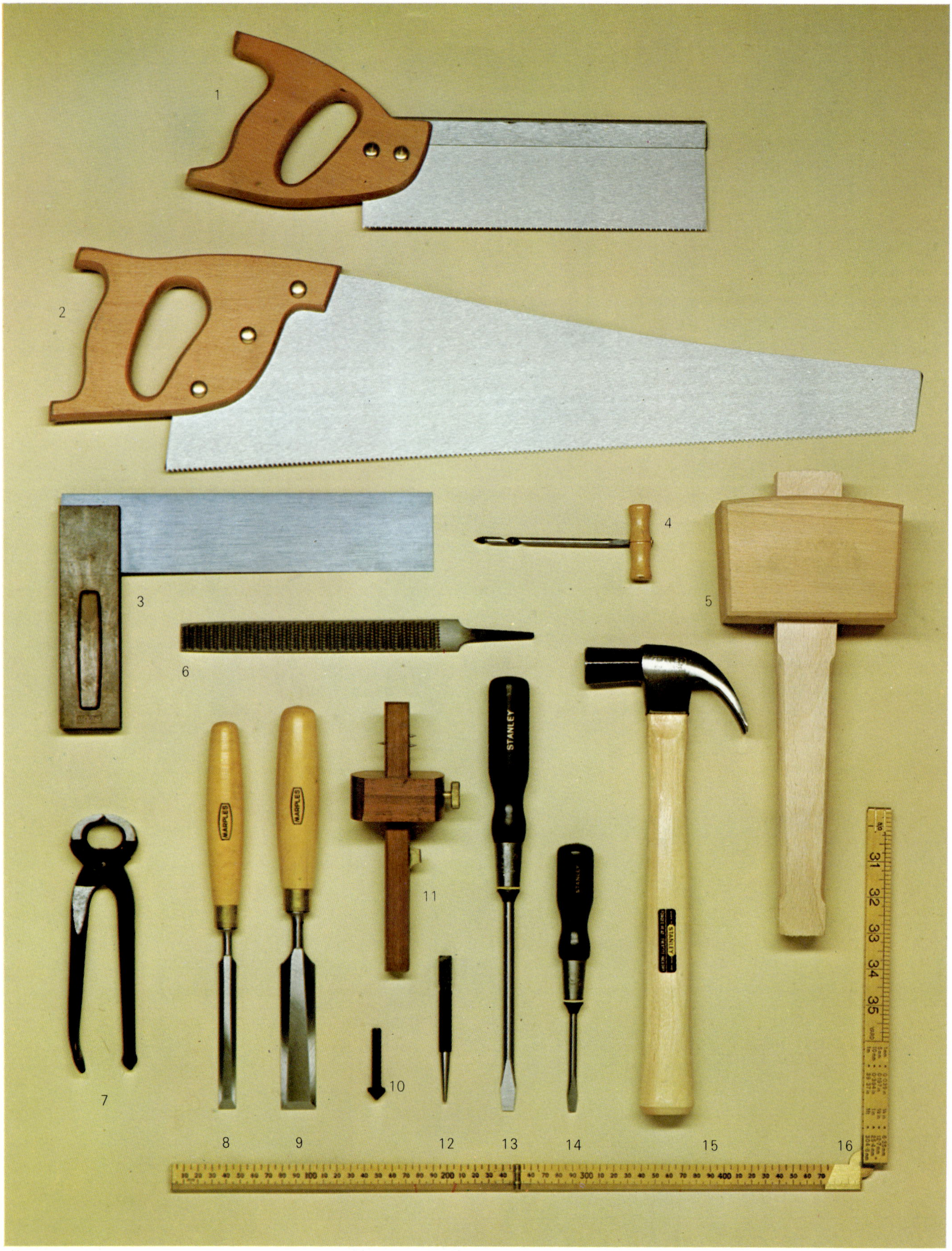
1
2
3
4
5
6
7
8
9
10
11
12
13
14
15
16
STANLEY

Left Woodworking tools: 1 Tenon saw, 2 Panel saw, 3 Set-square, 4 Gimlet, 5 Wooden mallet, 6 Rasp, 7 Pincers, 8 12 mm ($\frac{1}{2}$ in) wood chisel, 9 25 mm (1 in) wood chisel, 10 Countersink, 11 Mortise gauge, 12 Nail punch, 13, 14 Screwdrivers, 15 Claw hammer, 16 Folding rule.
Above Power tools: 1 Two-speed electric drill with 12 mm ($\frac{1}{2}$ in) chuck, 2 Masonry drills (to be used at the low-speed setting), 3 Set of high-speed twist drills, 4 Circular-saw attachment, 5 Rubber rotary sander attachment and sanding discs, 6 Orbital sander attachment.

Hardcore should always be well compacted so that it spreads the load from the top surface. A purchased or home-made rammer is required for this. If you make your own, ensure that it is reasonably heavy and that the base is not too broad. A sledgehammer may be necessary, too, to smash up old brick-ends into more convenient smaller sizes and for demolition.

Power tools

An electric drill is so versatile and makes light of so many jobs that it is an essential tool for every handyman, and not least for use in the garden. It is worth paying a few pounds extra for a two-speed type with a chuck capacity of not less than 12 mm ($\frac{1}{2}$ in); this will be powerful enough to drill holes in walls if you are installing outdoor water pipes. If you anticipate drilling holes in masonry a hammer-type drill will be helpful. Always complement your drill with a generous extension lead, preferably wound onto a cable drum. You will need a set of good quality high-speed twist drills from 3 mm ($\frac{1}{8}$ in) to 12 mm ($\frac{1}{2}$ in), a 6 mm ($\frac{1}{4}$ in) masonry drill (and also perhaps a larger one for drilling for pipework), and a countersink.

One of the most useful electric-drill attachments is the circular saw, which is an invaluable time-saver if you are cutting quantities of timber. Use a combination blade rather than a cross-cut blade if you are cutting sheets of plywood or natural timber parallel to the grain. Sanding attachments, both rotary and orbital, are useful for removing paint, cleaning up, and fine sanding. A small arbor grindstone will enable you to sharpen blunt drills.

The main disadvantage of having such numerous attachments for one tool is that you invariably find that you need to use the drill (for instance) immediately after using the saw. The obvious, although rather expensive, answer to the problem can be seen in the trend toward purpose-made tools – saws, hedgetrimmers, and a variety of other equipment – each with its built-in power source.

In the interests of safety, many drills today are of the double-insulated type, which requires no earth-wire connection. If your drill is not double insulated, it is essential that you fit it with a correctly fused three-pin plug.

Tool care

Most hand tools will last a lifetime if they are properly cared for – and that includes using them only for the jobs for which they were designed. Using a spade as a makeshift axe for cutting a large tree root is likely to result in a broken spade handle.

After every day's use tools should be thoroughly cleaned off and left dry or with a light covering of oil, as may be appropriate. Attend at once to any minor maintenance.

A well-organized tool shed or cupboard, in which tools are always returned to their appointed place, sounds like a counsel of perfection – but it is the only certain way of avoiding those infuriating moments when the chisel, or pliers, or screwdriver are needed quickly but cannot be found. The store should be kept as dry as possible to prevent steel equipment rusting. It is a good idea to bring your toolbox into the warmth and dryness of the house for the winter months.

Hiring equipment

Many of the projects in this book involve the use of expensive equipment for a limited period. The only way in which costs can be held down to a reasonable level in such projects is to hire the equipment. This has become much easier in recent years, and there are now well over 200 tool-hire shops in Britain. Most of these shops hire a wide range of do-it-yourself equipment, and many offer equipment as specialized as concrete mixers, angle grinders, post-hole borers, hammer drills, demolition hammers, and vibrating rollers.

Before hiring the more expensive equipment make a point of comparing the charges of different companies – they may vary significantly. Delivery and collection of the larger items is likely to cost extra. If you own, or can borrow, an estate car you will be able to collect and return, say, a small concrete mixer yourself – and, moreover, do so at times convenient to you.

Hiring costs can be minimized by careful planning to ensure that all preliminary work is completed beforehand and, if necessary, arranging that several jobs to be done by a particular tool are carried out at the same time. If you are unfamiliar with the operation of a particular mechanical tool, make sure that it is delivered with written instructions as to how to use it and, if possible, ask for a demonstration. Before accepting delivery, check it over for any signs of damage or malfunction or you may find yourself liable to pay for repairs for which you were not responsible. In particular, refuse to accept any mechanical or electrical equipment that is potentially unsafe. Safety goggles should be supplied with angle grinders; always use them when operating this equipment.

You will normally be expected to

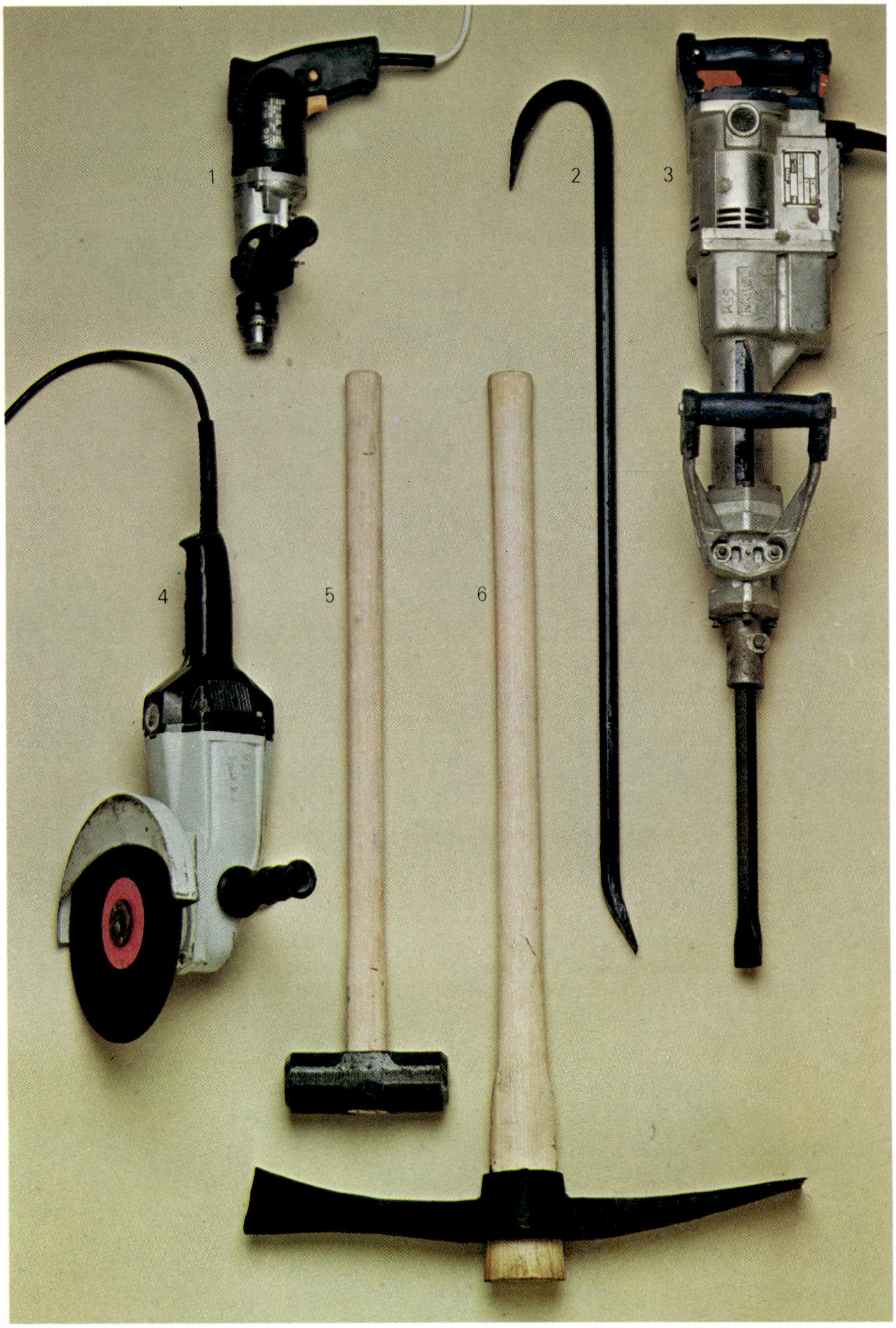

Specialized tools: 1 Hammer drill, 2 Small crowbar, 3 Drill for breaking concrete, 4 Powered angle grinder, 5 Sledge hammer, 6 Builder's pick.

Tools that can be hired: 1 Small concrete mixer, 2 Rammer, 3 Plate vibrator, 4 Hole-boring auger. These and other items are available from tool-hire shops.

make a deposit on the equipment, which will be refunded if the equipment is returned in a clean, undamaged condition. If the equipment is stolen while in your care, you will be expected to meet the replacement cost, so check your householder's insurance policy to see if it covers such a disaster.

Hiring is not invariably the cheapest way of dealing with the equipment problem. It may, for instance, be possible for you to buy some equipment secondhand, and it will certainly be worth your while to have a look at the classified advertisements in the trade and DIY journals. You may even be able to buy a concrete mixer in good working order for about one third of its cost when new. Such a price could be the equivalent of the cost of hiring a mixer for about five weeks. If you have a major concreting project this might be the cheaper way, since you would be able to sell the mixer when you had finished with it. Moreover, you would not have to worry about soaring hire charges if, for some reason, your concreting work was delayed.

Index

Acknowledgments

The publishers thank the following organisations and individuals for their kind permission to reproduce the photographs in this book:

A-Z Botanical Collection Limited 13 centre, 28 above right, 69 below left; Pat Brindley 24 below right, 41, 86; Camera Press Ltd 61; Cement and Concrete Association 55; Russell Coulart 8 above and below, 9 above; Ron and Christine Foord 50 above left; Brian Furner 53 above right, 66; Iris Hardwick Library 15, 54, 57 above, 84; John Harris 2, 24 above left, centre and right, 70, 71; Hozelock Limited 78, 79; Bill Mclaughlin 6, 87 above right; Mainspring Public Relations Limited 76; Marshalls of Halifax 60 above and below left and below right; *Practical Gardening* magazine 19, 34, 64, 65; David Prout 9 below, 17, 26, 28 below right, 31, 36, 37, 50 below right, 56, 57 below right, 72, 73, 85 above right; Malcolm Robertson 16, 91, 92, 93, 94, 95; Harry Smith Horticultural Photographic Collection 7, 10, 13 above and below left, 23, 29 above, 43, 47, 52, 63, 67; Spectrum Colour Library 81; Stapeley Water Gardens 68, 69 above left; Peter Stiles 75; Pamla Toler 1, 12, 18, 22, 25 above right, 27, 29 below right, 38, 44, 45, 48, 51 above right, 53 below left and right, 85 left; Michael Warren 25 below right; Elizabeth Whiting and Associates 5, 59 below, 61 above right, 87 below, 88.

The publishers thank Hire Service Shops and E. Amette & Co Ltd for the loan of tools photographed on pages 91, 92, 93, 94, 95.

Drawings: Advertising Arts 68, 73, 74, 76, 77, 78; David Bryant 10, 11, 39, 58; Venner Artists 12, 19, 20, 21, 22, 26, 32, 34, 35, 36, 40, 41, 42, 43, 49, 56, 83, 84, 86, 88, 89.